JUST A LITTLE GIRL FROM TAHLEQUAH: LISA CHRISTIANSEN'S JOURNEY TO THE WHITE HOUSE"

Book Description

"This book is a gripping photo-biography of the arduous journey Dr. Lisa Christine Christiansen took to make her way from almost having been aborted three times to becoming one of the most influential and controversial Native American Cherokee women from the United Keetoowah Band of Cherokee Indians in Oklahoma. Christiansen is born from the Keetoowah Nighthawk Society, blue people clan to a long lineage of historically significant women and men. Most notably, her 5th generation great-grandfather Sequoyah "George 'Gist' Guess" and NASA'S Mary Golda Ross - the first known Native American female engineer and the first female  engineer in the history of Lockheed. She was one of the 40 founding engineers of Lockheed's renowned and highly secretive Skunk Works project. Both are direct descendants of Christiansen's mother, Mary Ann

Groundhog. This book brings us through her arrival as one of few Executive Advisors to President Donald J. Trump and her continued support in the Trump Administration."

Dedication

I dedicate this book to my daddy, Mack Vann, who inspired me to chase and catch my dreams. To the United Keetoowah band of Cherokee Indians for always being a compass, reminding me of my deep roots as a member of the Keetoowah Nighthawk Society. To Habib Carouba for teaching me a business acumen that reaches beyond common thinking. He taught me everything in life is a negotiation and the importance of investing on your terms, living life on your terms, and that family isn't always blooded, and, of course, I give all glory to God.

Table of Contents

Chapter 1: A Birth Shrouded in Secrets

Chapter 2: Echoes of the Past

Chapter 3: A Legacy Unveiled

Chapter 4: A Journey Ignited

Chapter 5: Farewell to a Warrior

Chapter 6: A Shift in Perspective

Chapter 7: Dreams and Determination

Chapter 8: A Model's Odyssey

Chapter 9: Legacy of Greatness

Chapter 10: An Extraordinary Grandfather

Chapter 11: Defining Moments

Chapter 12: Keeler's Contributions to the Bill and OCCO's Dissent

Chapter 13: Legacy and Life after the OCCO Conflict

Chapter 14: A Journey of Vision and Determination

Chapter 15: The Unseen Side of Donald Trump

Chapter 16: A Journey into Politics

Chapter 17: Gratitude and Reminders

Chapter 1: A Birth Shrouded in Secrets

The year was 1966, and the air was thick with the mingling scents of fried food and livestock. The prison rodeo always brought a peculiar energy to our small town, an energy that buzzed with a mix of anticipation and forbidden thrill. As the sun dipped below the sky, casting a warm orange glow over the festivities, I couldn't help but feel that this particular September evening held something more than just the promise of daring stunts and raucous laughter.

Amidst the electric energy of the rodeo, Fayeola Spears stood beside my father, Mack Vann, his rugged features illuminated by the vivid carnival lights. Mack Vann and Fayeola Spears stood together near the grandstand of the make-shift rodeo arena. The light drizzle that had begun moments ago was a welcome relief from the day's heat, and the droplets seemed to dance in the air like shimmering diamonds.

Beside Mack Vann stood my aunt, Fayeola Spears – a woman of unwavering strength, her presence commanding respect even in this unlikely setting. Her laughter mingled with the distant roars of the crowd as she recounted stories of rodeos past, her animated gestures adding a touch of vibrancy to the cool evening air.

As the rodeo commenced, the first event unfolded before their eyes. Bull riders clung desperately to bucking beasts, defying the laws of gravity and reason. The cheers and gasps of the crowd echoed around them, creating a symphony of emotions that temporarily drowned out the surrounding walls of confinement.

During one of these heart-stopping moments, as a rider was dramatically thrown to the ground, a figure approached them – a Keetoowah Lighthorse Tribal Marshall with an envelope in hand. His stern expression betrayed no hint of the news he bore, yet the atmosphere shifted gradually. He handed the envelope to my father, saying, "You've got a message."

Mack's weathered hands trembled as he tore open the envelope, eyes scanning the contents. A hushed silence fell over Fayeola, a shroud of anticipation as she waited for Mack to reveal the message. Fayeola's eyes met Mack's, and Fayeola saw a mixture of curiosity and concern in his gaze.

Finally, Mack cleared his throat, his voice infused with disbelief and wonder as he read aloud the cryptic message that would alter the course of their lives. "Meet me where the river bends, where shadows dance upon the water. A revelation awaits, secrets to unfurl, destinies to be woven anew."

The words hung in the air, an enigma wrapped in intrigue. Questions buzzed in our minds like bees around honey – who had sent this message, and what secrets lay hidden, waiting to be unraveled? Fayeola's voice broke the silence, her tone steady despite the uncertainty. "We must go, Mack. The river has stories to tell, and it seems we are meant to be its audience."

And so, as the last rays of sunlight painted the prison walls with a golden hue, we made a silent pact to embark on this mysterious journey. The rodeo, once a beacon of fleeting escape, now paled compared to the adventure that awaited us at the river's bend. Destiny had whispered its call, and we were determined to heed it, regardless of where it might lead.

Little did we know, this whispered message marked the beginning of a journey that would unveil secrets shrouded in darkness and weave a tapestry of destinies that would forever bind our fates together?

The moon hung low on the horizon, casting a silvery glow over the world as the clock struck 2:00 am on that fateful September 4, 1966. It was a time when the world held its breath as if nature itself paused to witness the arrival of an enigmatic protagonist, Lisa Christiansen. Her entry into the world was not without its challenges; a fighter from the very beginning, she emerged as a preemie, her tiny form bearing the weight of an unsettling past.

As the ancestors before us watched from the corner of the dimly lit room, the soft glow of a distant light accentuated the moment's intensity. Mack's heart pounded in rhythm with the newborn's first cries, a symphony of life and hope that echoed through the air. Mary Ann Groundhog, the resilient mother, cradled her precious creation, her eyes reflecting a mixture of exhaustion and sheer determination. The bond between mother and child was palpable, a connection forged through trials and choices that defied convention.

"Welcome, little one," Mary Ann whispered, her voice a tender caress that seemed to bridge the gap between the past and the present. She brushed a gentle kiss against Lisa's forehead, a silent promise of protection and love. I stood there, a silent observer of this unfolding story, my heart stirred by the unspoken emotions that hung in the air.

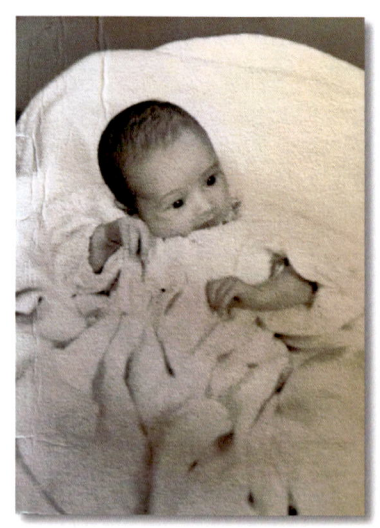

Mary Ann's gaze met mine as dawn began to break, casting a soft golden hue over the room. "This child, Mack, she's a fighter," she said, her voice carrying pride and exhaustion. "She'll defy the odds, just like her mother."

I nodded in agreement, my eyes fixed on the tiny bundle of life nestled in Mary Ann's arms. The weight of the past, the choices made in the shadows, seemed to linger in the air, casting a subtle veil of mystery over Lisa's arrival. Mary Ann's journey had been one of challenges and complexities, and now, as Lisa took her first breaths, it was as if the past and present converged in a single heartbeat.

The room seemed to hold its breath, a suspended moment in time, as Mary Ann cradled Lisa. "We'll protect her, won't we?" she asked, her voice tinged with vulnerability. "We'll give her a chance at a different life,

free from the shadows that have haunted us."

I stepped closer, my hand resting on Mary Ann's shoulder, a silent reassurance passing between us. "We'll do whatever it takes," I vowed, my voice steady with conviction. "Lisa will know love, strength, and the power to shape her destiny."

And so, in that quiet room illuminated by the soft glow of dawn, a pact was silently sealed – a promise to nurture and protect, to guide Lisa Christiansen through life as intricate as it was gripping. The enigma of her birth, the choices that had brought her to this moment, would become the foundation upon which her journey would unfold.

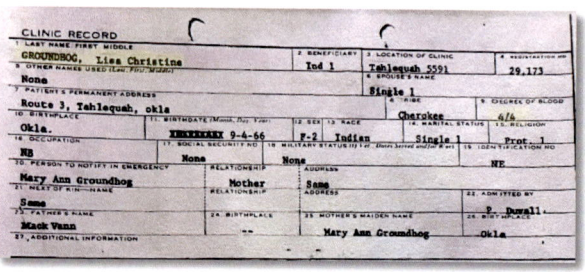

As the world outside awakened to a new day, we held onto the belief that despite the secrets that shrouded our pasts, a future of endless possibilities awaited the resilient soul that had entered our lives. The tale of Lisa Christiansen had begun, and it was destined to be as captivating as the soft September breeze that had whispered the news of her arrival.

Amidst the uncertainties, one steadfast presence stood out like a beacon of hope. My father, Mack Vann, a man of resolute character and unwavering love, emerged as a guardian angel during the most trying times. His stories of dedication and sacrifice wove a vivid tapestry of an extraordinary bond that would shape our lives.

In the calm corners of our humble abode, Mack's voice took on a soothing cadence as he recounted the tale of Lisa's battle with whooping cough. I sat on the edge of my seat, captivated by his words as they painted a picture of resilience and unwavering determination.

"It was a bitterly cold winter," Mack began, his gaze distant as if reliving the memories himself. "Lisa was just a few months old, and the cough had taken hold of her fragile body. Each night was a battle, her small chest heaving as she fought for each precious breath."

My heart ached at the thought of that tiny, vulnerable infant struggling against the cruel grip of illness. "What did you do, Mack?" I asked, my voice barely a whisper as I hung on his every word.

Mack's eyes met mine, and a soft smile tugged at the corners of his lips. "I held her close, just like this," he said, cradling an imaginary bundle in his arms. "I rocked her repeatedly, whispering words of strength and love. I refused to let her give up, and I could see the spark of fight in those tiny eyes."

His hands moved with a tenderness that belied his rugged exterior, and I marveled at the depth of his love and commitment. "There were nights when I thought we might lose her," Mack continued, his voice tinged with emotion. "But I was determined to be her anchor, her lifeline in the storm."

The room seemed to fade as Mack's narrative unfolded, leaving only the two of us in a cocoon of shared memories. His stories painted a vivid picture of his sleepless nights, his unwavering presence by Lisa's side, and the countless moments when he had whispered words of encouragement into the darkness.

"And then, one morning," Mack's voice grew softer, his eyes glistening with unshed tears, "I heard it – a faint, steady rhythm. Lisa's cough had subsided, replaced by the sweet sound of peaceful breathing. It was as if the universe itself exhaled a sigh of relief."

I wiped away a tear that had escaped my eye, moved by the sheer strength of Mack's devotion. "You saved her," I whispered, my voice choking with emotion.

Mack nodded, his gaze never leaving mine. "But she saved me too," he said, whispering. "At that moment, I realized that our bond was unbreakable. We were connected by a thread of love and resilience, a bond that nothing could sever."

As Mack's story ended, a profound silence settled between us, the weight of his words sinking in. The foundation of their unbreakable connection had been laid during those harrowing days of illness, a testament to a father's unwavering love and a child's indomitable spirit.

Amid the enigmatic circumstances surrounding Lisa's birth and the secrets that shrouded our past, Mack's tale stood as a testament to the power of love and dedication. It was a reminder that even in the face of uncertainty, there were moments of profound clarity – moments when the depth of our connections illuminated the path ahead, guiding us through the labyrinth of life's mysteries.

Amidst the layers of intrigue surrounding our lives, one figure stood out as a multi-faceted enigma, commanding attention and curiosity. My mother, Mary Ann Groundhog, a woman of captivating beauty and a fierce spirit, held within her the complexities of a dual nature that defied easy understanding. Her legacy, woven with remarkable achievements and enigmatic actions, cast a shadow of admiration and mystery.

The mention of Mary Ann's name conjured an aura of respect and awe. "Your mother," Mack would often say, his voice a mix of reverence and admiration, "was a force to be reckoned with." I hung onto his every 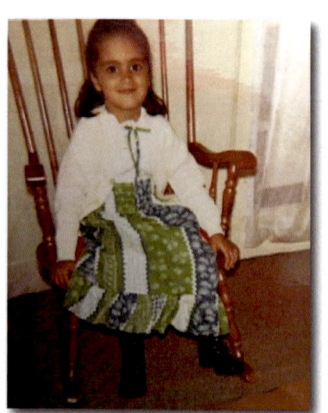 word, eager to uncover the layers that made up this complex woman who had birthed me.

During one of my rare visits with Mary Ann, I caught a glimpse of her spirited nature. As I walked into the room, her presence was undeniable – a whirlwind of energy that seemed to fill every corner. "Lisa," she exclaimed, her voice bringing warmth and vitality. "You've grown into a fine young woman." I was only seven years old.

I couldn't help but feel a surge of pride at her words, a sense of validation that only a mother's approval could bring. "Momma, you're here!" I replied, my voice tinged with mixed emotions. "Please stay, please."

Mary Ann's gaze softened, and for a moment, the walls that had always seemed to separate us melted away. "Life has its twists and turns, my dear," she said, her tone tinged with a hint of sadness. "But know I've always been watching from a distance, cheering you on."

Her words struck a chord deep within me, a realization that our connection, though fleeting, was rooted in a shared bond. It was a bond that extended beyond our shared physical moments, transcending time and space. At that moment, the enigmatic aura that had always surrounded Mary Ann seemed to lift, revealing a mother who cared deeply, even if her actions often remained mysterious.

I continued to uncover fragments of Mary Ann's legacy – stories of co-founding the American Indian Movement and orchestrating victories against injustice that had shaped history. Her achievements were a testament to her indomitable spirit, her ability to channel her tempestuous nature into a force for change.

Yet, for all her outward strength, I couldn't help but wonder about the contrasting duality beneath the surface. "Tell me more about Mom," I once asked my daddy, Mack Vann, my curiosity getting the best of me.

Mack's eyes held a mixture of fondness and understanding. "Your mother was a puzzle, Lisa," he replied, his voice tinged with nostalgia. "She had a way of keeping her thoughts and emotions close to her chest, revealing what she wanted the world to see."

And so, the enigma of Mary Ann Groundhog continued to unravel before me, each piece of the puzzle revealing a new facet of her complex nature. Our encounters remained rare, our conversations fleeting, but the moments we shared held a depth of meaning that transcended the limits of time. As I navigated the intricacies of her legacy, I couldn't help but feel a growing sense of appreciation for the spirited mother who had shaped my journey, even from afar.

Chapter 2: Echoes of the Past

The memory of that day remains etched in my mind like a vivid painting – a snapshot of innocence and anticipation captured in the soft light of a summer afternoon. I stood in front of the mirror, adorned in a new dress that seemed to shimmer in the sunlight, shoes that felt a bit too big for my feet, and a "white" hairstyle that I had insisted on, hoping to emulate the elegance of the older girls in my school. My heart raced with excitement and nervousness, my tiny fingers adjusting the delicate ribbon in my hair.

Mack's voice broke through my thoughts, his warm smile reflecting in the mirror. "You look like a princess, Lisa," he said, his eyes gleaming with pride. "Ready for your big adventure?"

I nodded eagerly, my heart fluttering with a sense of anticipation. "Yes, Daddy! I can't wait to see her."

A note lay on the table, a secret plea concealed within its folds. As Mack handed it to me, I felt a tug at my heartstrings, a mix of curiosity and apprehension. Unfolding the paper, my eyes scanned the carefully penned words, each letter a testament to a desperate cry for connection. "Mom, I miss you. Please come see me," I whispered, my voice barely above a whisper.

Mack's gaze softened as he watched me read the note. "Your mother, Lisa," he began, his voice gentle, "she had her reasons for her choices. But remember, you're loved, and I'll always be here for you."

With a reassuring smile from Mack, I slipped the note into my pocket, determination sparking in my eyes. "I know, Daddy. But I want to understand; I want to know her."

And so, with the note clenched tightly in my hand, I embarked on a journey that would lead me to a fateful encounter, a revelation that would shake my world to its very core. As I  walked down the familiar path, my heart pounded with excitement and trepidation, the weight of the secrets that lay ahead heavy on my shoulders.

The sun cast long shadows as I arrived at the designated meeting spot, my eyes scanning the surroundings with hope and uncertainty. And then, like a phantom from the past, she appeared – Mary Ann Groundhog, the woman who had given me life. Her presence was both haunting and comforting, an echo of the past intertwined with the reality of the present.

"Mama," I whispered, my voice filled with longing and emotion.

Mary Ann's gaze met mine, her eyes reflecting a complex array of emotions – regret, sadness, and a touch of surprise. "Lisa," she said, her voice a mere whisper. "I didn't think you'd come."

I held up the note, my voice trembling with the weight of unspoken questions. "You left this. I had to come."

As our eyes locked, a torrent of emotions surged between us, the unspoken words hanging in the air like a fragile thread. And then, in a voice of sincerity, Mary Ann began to weave the tale of her abandonment, which would forever reshape my understanding of the past and the secrets that had shrouded our lives.

The world around us seemed to fade away, leaving only the two of us in a cocoon of shared confessions. Raw and genuine, the truth tumbled, carrying a sense of catharsis and vulnerability. And as the echoes of the past reverberated through our conversation, I realized that this encounter marked a pivotal moment. This turning point would shape the trajectory of our lives in ways I could never have imagined, even at eight years old.

The photograph I held seemed to hold the key to a world

 of mysteries and untold stories. As the image captured the fleeting smiles and shared moments of my mother and stepfather, Steve Eslinger, I felt a chill run down my spine. It was as if the very essence of their relationship was captured within the frame, a silent witness to a truth that had remained concealed for so long.

Days turned into weeks, and the aftershocks of that photograph reverberated through my life. Steve Eslinger stepped into my world, casting an enigmatic shadow over the unfolding events. He was a man of few words, his eyes carrying a weight of unspoken experiences. Yet, there was a kindness in his gaze, a gentle reassurance that made me feel I could confide in him.

"Lisa," he said one evening, his voice tinged with empathy and caution, "there are things you deserve to know. Your mother, she didn't just disappear. There's more to the story."

I felt a knot tighten in my stomach as I listened, my heart racing with curiosity and apprehension. "What happened?" I asked, my voice barely above a whisper.

He hesitated as if carefully choosing his words. "Your parents, they weren't like any ordinary couple," he began, his gaze distant as if reliving the past. "There was a rift between them that ran deep and unspoken. Your mother, she fled back to Oklahoma, leaving you behind."

The words hit me like a wave, a chilling reality that sent shivers down my spine. My mother, the woman who had brought me into this world, had left me behind without a second thought for a second time once when I was born, and now this. I struggled to comprehend the magnitude of her actions and the complexity of her choices that had shaped my life.

"And there's more," Steve continued, his voice laden with sadness and resignation. "Before she left, there was an incident. Your mother, she injured me, Lisa. It was a moment of rage, and it left its mark."

The room seemed to close in around me as I processed his words. My mother, the spirited enigma, had inflicted harm upon the man I had just met. The memory of that injury lingered, intertwining with the complex emotions that shaped my early experiences.

As days turned into weeks, the weight of the truth bore down on me, a burden that felt almost suffocating. I found solace in the conversations with my daddy, Mack Vann; his presence was a source of comfort and unease. He became more than my daddy; he became a confidante, a man who had witnessed the unraveling of a relationship and the aftermath of its storm.

"Lisa," he said one evening, his voice soft yet filled with conviction, "the path ahead won't be easy. But you're stronger than you know. You have the power to shape your destiny, to rise above the echoes of the past."

His words resonated within me, a spark of hope amid the turmoil. And as I looked back on the moments that had led me to this point – the photographs, the conversations, the revelations – I realized that each piece of the puzzle had brought me closer to understanding the enigmatic tapestry of my past.

The echoes of the past reverberated through my thoughts, a constant reminder of the choices that had shaped my journey. And as I navigated the labyrinth of emotions and revelations, I couldn't help but wonder what lay ahead, what secrets were still waiting to be uncovered, and how the complexities of my history would continue to shape the person I was becoming.

Amidst the uncertainty that had swept into my life, an unexpected pillar of strength emerged – my Aunt Fayeola. With limited resources and a determination that knew no bounds, she stepped into the role of protector and provider, navigating the challenges of raising me with an unwavering love that defied the odds.

Fayeola's presence was a constant reassurance, a guiding light in the darkness that had enveloped our lives. "Lisa," she said one evening, her voice carrying a mix of tenderness and resolve, "we may not have much, but we have each other. And that's enough."

I nodded, my heart swelling with gratitude for the woman who had become a mother figure in my life. "I know, Aunt Fay. I'm just scared sometimes."

She reached out and gently squeezed my hand, her touch a source of comfort. "Fear is a part of life, my Little Lizard. But we don't let it define us. We rise above it together."

And rise we did, navigating life's challenges with a resilience that seemed to flow through our veins. Fayeola's determination knew no bounds as she worked tirelessly to provide for us, her sacrifices a testament to the depths of her love. She juggled multiple jobs, always with a smile and a twinkle in her eyes that spoke of hope and unwavering resolve.

Yet, amidst the struggles and triumphs, there existed a reminder of the harrowing encounters that had shaped our bond – an indelible scar on my arm, a tangible mark of Fayeola's protective nature. "Lisa," she said one day, her voice a mixture of sorrow and determination, "I'll do whatever it takes to keep you safe."

I traced the scar with my fingers, the memory of that fateful day still vivid. It had been a day like any other until a confrontation had escalated into a dangerous situation. The glint of a butcher knife, a flash of fear in Fayeola's eyes, and then a surge of adrenaline as she shielded me from harm. I was only eight years old.

"You saved my life," I whispered, my voice tinged with awe and gratitude.

Fayeola's gaze met mine, her eyes filled with pride and vulnerability. "You're my family, Lisa. I would do anything to protect you."

Our unbreakable bond solidified then, a connection forged through shared struggles, sacrifices, and the unwavering love that had sustained us. Fayeola had become more than just an aunt – she was a beacon of strength, inspiration, and a constant reminder that even in the face of adversity, love could conquer all.

Fayeola continued to be the steadfast presence in my life, a force that guided me through the twists and turns of our shared journey. Her unwavering love, determination, and the memory of that scar on my arm reminded me of the lengths she would go to protect me, to ensure that I would never have to face the storms of life alone.

And so, amidst the trials and triumphs, the scars and the unspoken words, Fayeola and I navigated the mysteries of our past, the echoes of the stories that had shaped us, and the unbreakable bond that would forever anchor us in a sea of uncertainty.

My mother's legacy, Mary Ann Groundhog, was a tapestry woven with threads of both triumph and complexity. As I delved into her history, her activism, and alliances with influential figures such as Ronald Reagan  and Ted Kennedy painted a portrait of a woman of immense strength and unyielding ambition. Yet, behind the façade of her remarkable accomplishments, I discovered the intricate layers of her multi-faceted character – a juxtaposition of fierce determination and inner struggles that seemed to define her very existence.

I sat in the dimly lit room, surrounded by stacks of documents and faded photographs that chronicled Mary Ann's journey. "Tell me more about Mom," I had asked Daddy one day, a fire of curiosity burning within me.

He sighed, his gaze distant as if he were peering into the past. "Your mother, Lisa," he began, his voice tinged with admiration and complexity, "was a force to be reckoned with. She co-founded the American Indian Movement, stood alongside influential leaders, and fought for justice."

As Daddy's words vividly depicted Mary Ann's activism, I couldn't help but be in awe of the woman who had shaped my existence. Her strength, unrelenting commitment to her ideals, and ability to make her voice heard in a world that often ignored her spoke volumes about her character.

And yet, the story didn't end there. "But had her struggles, too," Daddy continued, his tone softening. "She battled with her inner demons, faced contradictions that seemed to tear at her soul."

I furrowed my brow, my curiosity piqued by the mention of inner struggles beneath the surface. "What kind of contradictions?" I asked, my voice barely above a whisper.

Daddy hesitated as if choosing his words carefully. "Your mother was a warrior for justice, but she also had moments of doubt. There were times when her actions seemed at odds with her beliefs when she grappled with the complexities of her choices."

As I continued to explore the legacy of Mary Ann Groundhog, I found myself drawn into a narrative that was as intricate as it was captivating. Her accomplishments and alliances with influential figures told one side of the story – a side that showcased her unyielding strength and ambition. Yet, her inner struggles, her contradictions, and the battles within her revealed another layer that made her undeniably human, relatable in ways I hadn't anticipated.

Reflecting on my mother's impact, I couldn't help but draw inspiration from the enduring strength that seemed to run in my veins. The legacy she had left behind was a reminder that even in the face of complexities and inner turmoil, it was possible to make a difference, stand up for what one believed in, and leave an indelible mark on the world.

And so, amidst the pages of history, the faded photographs, and the whispered tales, I discovered the woman who was both my mother and an enigma. Her journey was a mosaic of triumphs and contradictions, a reminder that the mysteries of the past could shape the present and inspire the future. As I continued to unravel the layers of her story, I couldn't help but wonder how her legacy would continue to shape my path, propelling me forward with an enduring sense of purpose and determination.

Each thread revealed a new layer of relationships and emotions that had woven together to shape the journey I found myself on. It was as if I were peering through a window into a world of longing and complexities, each revelation sparking a sense of intrigue and mystery.

One day, as I sifted through old photographs, I came across an image that seemed to hold a story all its own. In it, my mother stood beside a man whose eyes were warm and uncertain. "Who is this?" I asked Fayeola. My voice tinged with curiosity.

She sighed, her gaze fixed on the photograph. "That's David," she replied, her voice soft. "Your mother's last love."

My heart skipped a beat as I absorbed the information. "What happened to him?"

Fayeola's eyes held a mixture of sorrow and understanding. "Their love was fierce, but life took them in different directions. David left, and your mother moved on."

As I stared at the photograph, I couldn't help but feel a pang of sadness for the love that had been lost. The stories left untold. It was a reminder that even amidst the triumphs and complexities, moments of vulnerability and heartache shaped the tapestry of our lives.

Amidst the turbulence of my journey, the bravery of my daddy, Mack Vann, became a cornerstone of resilience. "Lisa," he said one evening, his voice carrying a mix of determination and pride, "we may face challenges, but we face them together."

I nodded, a sense of unity and strength washing over me. 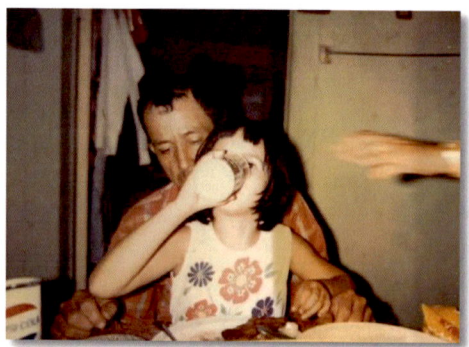 "You're right, Daddy. We've come this far, and we'll keep moving forward."

His reassuring smile spoke volumes, a silent promise of unwavering support that gave me the courage to face whatever lay ahead. And alongside his bravery, there existed the protective instincts of my aunt Fayeola, a woman whose sacrifices and love had become an unbreakable foundation.

"Lisa," Fayeola said one day, her voice a mixture of tenderness and conviction, "we've faced storms before, and we'll weather them again. You're not alone in this."

Her words resonated within me, a reminder that the strength of our bonds held together the complexities of our past. We forged a path forward, united by a shared history and an unbreakable connection.

Amidst it all, my mother's legacy, Mary Ann Groundhog, painted a portrait of a lady who defied convention and left a permanent mark on the tapestry of my life. Her triumphs and contradictions, fierce determination, and inner struggles all contributed to the enigma that was her character. And as I reflected on the legacy she had left behind, I couldn't help but feel a sense of reverence for the woman who had shaped my existence.

The tapestry of my past continued to unfurl before me, each thread interweaving with the next to form a captivating and mysterious story. And as I navigated the twists and turns, the triumphs and heartaches, I realized that the echoes of the past guided me towards a future that was uniquely my own – a lot shaped by the complexities of my history and the enduring strength that ran through my veins.

Chapter 3: A Legacy Unveiled

Tahlequah, where the whispers of my Cherokee lineage danced through the air like a melody, held within its embrace the echoes of my past and the promise of an extraordinary journey that awaited me. As I stood at the crossroads of my heritage and an unexpected path, the weight of generations seemed to rest upon my shoulders. The legacy of Sequoyah, the visionary creator of the Cherokee alphabet, wove an intricate thread through the tapestry of my life.

It was a crisp autumn morning when I stood before the gates of the White House, a place that held both power and history in its very stones. The journey from Tahlequah to this iconic symbol of American democracy felt like a testament to the enduring spirit of my ancestors. This spirit had overcome trials and tribulations, carrying a strength that defied the passage of time.

"Lisa, are you ready?" Daddy's voice broke through my thoughts, his presence a reassuring anchor as we prepared to enter a world of intrigue and possibility.

I took a deep breath, my heart fluttering with excitement and nerves. "I think so, Daddy. Let's do this."

As we entered the White House, the air seemed to crackle with anticipation, and I couldn't help but feel a sense of  awe at the history surrounding me. Our visit aimed to introduce ourselves and share our story with those who held the power to shape the future. And at the heart of that story was the legacy of Sequoyah, the man who had gifted the Cherokee people with a written language.

As I began to speak, the words flowed like a river, carrying the weight of generations. "I am Lisa from the Blue People Clan, a native of the United Keetoowah Band of Cherokee Indians and a little girl from Tahlequah. I carry the legacy of Sequoyah," I said, my voice steady and unwavering. "His vision, his creation of the Cherokee alphabet, symbolizes the strength of our ancestry and the power of our voice."

The room seemed to hang on my every word, the silence pregnant with anticipation. And as I continued to share the tale of my rich Cherokee lineage, the remarkable achievements of my mother, and the resilience of those who had come before me, I felt a sense of purpose that transcended the moment.

"Our heritage is a tapestry woven with threads of triumph and complexity," I continued, my gaze sweeping across the faces before me. "It is a reminder that our circumstances do not define us, but by the choices we make and the legacy we leave behind."

The depth of my heritage took center stage, casting a spotlight on the journey that led me to this moment. I spoke of the challenges faced by my family, the sacrifices made, and the unbreakable bonds that had sustained us through the storms of life. And with each word, I could feel the weight of generations – the legacy of Sequoyah, the bravery of my grandfather, George Washington Groundhog, the protective instincts of my aunt, and the enigmatic spirit of my mother – all converging to shape the remarkable tale that lay ahead.

A sense of reverence settled over the room, the echoes of my words hanging in the air like a promise of what was to come. And as I stepped away from the podium, a profound sense of gratitude washed over me – gratitude for the journey that had brought me here, for the legacy that had been unveiled, and for the opportunity to carry forward the spirit of my ancestors into a future that held boundless possibilities.

My journey found its genesis after my mother's passing, a transformative event that began a new phase in my life. The weight of her absence hung heavy in the air, and as I navigated the sea of emotions that followed, my father's poignant words became a guiding light amidst the darkness.

"Lisa," he said one evening, his voice carrying a mixture of sadness and determination, "you are a phoenix rising from the ashes of silence. Your mother's legacy lives on within you, and you have the power to shape a destiny that defies the odds."

His words resonated within me, a spark of hope that illuminated the path ahead. I knew that my mother's

complex history cast a shadow that extended far beyond her physical presence, and the mysteries that had shrouded her life ignited a quest within me – a quest for healing, understanding, and the truth that had remained elusive for so long.

As I delved into the pages of history, retracing the footsteps of my mother's journey, I uncovered layers of complexity that both intrigued and haunted me. Conversations with those who had known her painted a portrait of a woman who was both enigmatic and magnetic, a force of nature that had left an indelible mark on those who had crossed her path.

"People say your mother was a force to be reckoned with," Daddy said many times, his voice tinged with respect and nostalgia. "She had a way of commanding attention, of leaving her imprint wherever she went."

I nodded, my mind swirling with a mixture of emotions. "I want to understand, Daddy. I want to uncover the truths that have remained hidden."

He placed a hand on my shoulder, his gaze steady and reassuring. "Remember, Lisa, sometimes the truth is a puzzle with missing pieces. But that doesn't mean you can't create your picture."

His words echoed in my thoughts as I continued my quest for answers. My mother's legacy, triumphs, and contradictions seemed to dance just beyond my reach, a tantalizing enigma that beckoned me forward.

And as the days turned into nights and the pages of history unfurled before me, I realized that my journey was more than just a search for answers – it was a quest for healing, a way to connect the threads of my past and weave them into a narrative that would shape my present and future.

My mother's legacy influenced me, igniting a fire within my heart that burned with an earnest determination. As I embarked on this mysterious journey of discovery, I couldn't help but feel that I was stepping into the shadows of the past, each step bringing me closer to unraveling the mysteries that had defined my family's story.

Amid it all, I clung to my father's words, the image of a phoenix rising from the ashes as a powerful reminder of the strength that ran through my veins. The path ahead was shrouded in uncertainty but armed with my mother's legacy and the unyielding determination to uncover the truth. I was ready to embrace challenges and shape a destiny that defied the odds.

The shroud of family secrets began to lift, revealing a tapestry woven with threads of pain and redemption. As I delved deeper into the annals of history, the stories that emerged were heartbreaking and inspiring, a mosaic of tragedy and transgressions, yet buoyed by forgiveness and the unwavering pursuit of grace.

The story of my mother, her life, a complex dance of triumphs and contradictions, became a cornerstone of my quest. "Tell me more about Grandma," I asked Fayeola one day, my voice tinged with curiosity.

Fayeola's gaze softened, her eyes reflecting nostalgia and sorrow. "Your grandmother, Lisa, was a survivor. She faced hardships that would have broken many, but she held onto her faith and belief in forgiveness's power."

As Fayeola shared the tale of my grandmother's journey, I couldn't help but be captivated by the resilience that had carried her through life's darkest moments. The pain she had endured and the sacrifices she had made were all testaments to the strength that ran through our veins. A power passed down through generations.

And then there was the story of my aunt, a woman whose

 protective instincts and unwavering love had shaped my upbringing. "Aunt Fay," I asked, my voice filled with curiosity, "tell me about your journey."

She smiled, a mixture of fondness and reflection in her eyes. "My journey, Lisa, has been one of challenges and triumphs. I've faced setbacks but also witnessed the beauty of second chances and the power of redemption."

I marveled at the intricacies of her life – the hurdles she had overcome, the moments of grace that had transformed her path, and the unbreakable bond she had forged with me. Her journey was a testament to the resilience that coursed through our veins, a resilience that had carried us through the storms of life and would continue to shape our destiny.

As the puzzle pieces fell into place, I couldn't help but be struck by the profound interconnectedness of our lives.

The pain and redemption that had shaped my family's story were woven together in a tapestry that spanned generations, showcasing the intricate layers of our existence and the enduring strength that bound us together.

And so, as the shroud of family secrets continued to lift, the stories of my mother, grandmother, and aunt came to light, each narrative a reflection of the human experience – a dance of joy and sorrow, triumphs and transgressions, forgiveness and grace. As I navigated the twists and turns of their journeys, I couldn't help but feel a profound sense of gratitude for the legacy they had left behind – a legacy that had shaped my path and instilled within me a sense of purpose and determination.

The tapestry of our family's history was a mosaic of emotions and experiences, a reminder that even amidst the shadows of the past existed a resilient spirit that refused to be broken. And as I continued to unravel the mysteries that had defined our lives, I knew that this quest for understanding, healing, and grace would ultimately lead me to a place of profound transformation, where the echoes of the past would pave the way for a future that held boundless possibilities.

I grappled with myriad emotions – pain, understanding, and a profound sense of purpose. The stories in the shadows were now laid bare, their complexities a testament to the human experience and the depths of our shared humanity.

Amid it all, I embraced the transformative power of forgiveness and gratitude. "Aunt Fay," I said one evening, my voice tinged with newfound clarity, "I understand now. Forgiveness is a gift we give ourselves, a way to break free from the chains of the past."

Fayeola's eyes sparkled with pride and understanding. "You've learned a valuable lesson, Lisa. Forgiveness is not about condoning the actions of others. It's about releasing the hold that pain has on our hearts."

As I embarked on my healing journey, I was weaving a tapestry of forgiveness that stretched across generations. The pain of the past began to lose its grip, replaced by a sense of understanding and compassion that allowed me to see my loved ones as flawed yet resilient individuals who had navigated the complexities of their own lives.

In the quiet moments of reflection, I felt the presence of those who had come before me, their spirits lingering like whispers in the wind. "Mom," I whispered one night, staring at the moonlit sky, "I hope you've found peace. Your legacy lives on, and I'm determined to honor it."

The path to healing became a testament to the unbreakable bonds of love that persisted beyond the veil of mortality. Each step I took, each choice I made, felt like a tribute to the resilience of those who had shaped my journey – my mother, my grandmother, my aunt, and the generations that came before them.

Amidst the darkness of uncertainty, I found solace in believing that my loved ones had found the peace they sought. Their stories, struggles, and triumphs had become a part of me, shaping my narrative in ways I had never imagined.

And so, with a heart filled with gratitude for the lessons learned and the legacy uncovered, I embarked on a new journey to honor the memory of those who had paved the way for my existence. As I looked to the future, I carried with me the echoes of the past, a guiding light that illuminated my path and instilled a sense of purpose and determination.

The revelations of my family's history had ignited a fire within my heart that burned with the sincere desire to leave a legacy of my own – a gift of resilience, forgiveness, and the unwavering belief that love could transcend even the darkest of shadows. And as I walked this path of healing and understanding, I couldn't help but feel that the mysteries of the past had led me to a place of profound transformation, where the power of forgiveness and the enduring bonds of love would shape the tapestry of my own life in ways that were both remarkable and enduring.

Chapter 4: A Journey Ignited

My childhood unfolded against the backdrop of Briggs Elementary School in Oklahoma, a place where language barriers and cultural differences wove together to create a unique tapestry of experiences. Amidst the corridors and classrooms, a sense of normalcy enveloped me, but beneath the surface lay a world that was anything but ordinary.

"Lisa, are you excited for your first day of school?" Fayeola asked, her eyes filled with a mixture of anticipation and pride.

I nodded eagerly, my heart fluttering with excitement and nervousness. "I can't wait, Aunt Fayeola!"

As I entered the bustling schoolyard, laughter, and chatter filled the air. My immersion in the Cherokee language, a gift from my mother and a testament to our rich heritage set me apart in a sea of English speakers. Yet, rather than feeling isolated, I found myself drawn into a world that was both familiar and comforting.

The Cherokee language became the thread that connected me to my roots, a source of identity that cast a veil of normalcy over the complexities of my life. Conversations with classmates and stories shared with friends unfolded in the cadence of a language that was part of my very being.

"Lisa, can you help us with this word?" one of my classmates asked, holding up a book that featured both English and Cherokee text.

I smiled, eager to assist. "Of course! That word is 'tsalagi,' which means Cherokee."

As I navigated the corridors of Briggs Elementary School, I realized that my childhood was marked by a sense of innocence and curiosity that shielded me from the more profound complexities beyond the school walls. The whispers of my family's past and the mysteries that had ignited my journey were all present, yet somehow distant, as if the innocence of youth served as a protective shield.

"Lisa, we're learning about Sequoyah today," my teacher announced one morning, her voice filled with enthusiasm.

I sat up straighter. My heart swells with pride for my ancestor. "Sequoyah created the Cherokee alphabet," I said, a sense of ownership and connection infusing my words.

The classroom buzzed with excitement as we delved into the history of Sequoyah and the impact of the Cherokee syllabary. As I shared my own stories and experiences, I couldn't help but feel a profound sense of gratitude for the heritage that had shaped my identity.

And so, amidst the halls of Briggs Elementary School, a journey was ignited – a trip that would carry me beyond childhood innocence and into a world where the complexities of my family's history would become the sharper focus. But for now, as I laughed with friends, engaged in the vibrant culture of my people, and reveled in the joy of learning, the mysteries of the past remained a distant echo, a tale yet to be fully unveiled.

A poignant memory of my last conversation with my mother lingers, captured forever in a photograph from my time at Briggs Elementary. Like a precious gem hidden amidst the sands of time, the memory remains etched in my heart, a testament to the significance of our bond and the love that transcended distance and time.

The day was exciting as the school prepared for picture day. My classmates and I fidgeted with our hair, adjusted our outfits, and exchanged nervous glances. Amidst the anticipation, a sense of nostalgia washed over me – a reminder of the conversations my mother and I had shared during these moments in years past.

"Mom, I wish you were here to help me choose my outfit," I said, wistfully tinging my words as I held up two dresses for Fayeola's approval.

Fayeola smiled, her eyes holding a mixture of understanding and reassurance. "Your mom's spirit is always with you, Lisa. She's watching over you, guiding you."

I nodded, my heart filled with a sense of comfort. "I know. I miss her so much."

As I posed for the camera, the echoes of that conversation seemed to dance in the air around me, the memory etching itself into the fabric of time. It was a bittersweet moment, a glimpse into the profound love that had shaped my understanding of life and faith.

"Okay, Lisa, give me your best smile!" the photographer encouraged, his words breaking through my reverie.

I obliged, offering a smile that held within it a mixture of hope and longing. The camera clicked, capturing the essence of that moment – the innocence of youth, the anticipation of the future, and the unbreakable bond that connected me to my mother, even in her absence.

As I held the photograph in my hands, the image of my younger self staring back at me, I couldn't help but feel a sense of gratitude for the conversations we had shared, the memories we had created, and the love that had woven itself into the very fabric of my being.

Through the lens of that childhood memory, I glimpsed the profound truth that love was a force that transcended time and space. My mother's words, guidance, and the unwavering faith that had defined her existence were all present at that moment, a reminder that her legacy lived on within me.

And so, as I carried that photograph with me, a tangible reminder of the bond that connected us, I embarked on a journey rooted in the past and reaching toward the future. The innocence of childhood had shielded me from the complexities that lay beneath the surface, but within that innocence, I found a source of strength and understanding that would guide me through the mysteries that awaited.

As I looked at the photograph one last time, a smile tugged at the corners of my lips. The journey had only just begun, and through the lens of that poignant memory, I was reminded that the love that had shaped my past would continue to light the path ahead, illuminating the way toward a destiny that was uniquely my own.

The unexpected news of my mother's passing cast a shadow over my world, plunging me into a realm of profound sorrow and introspection. The reality of loss unfolded before me, a spectrum of emotions that spanned from denial to acceptance, each step a testament to the fragile nature of existence.

The phone call came on a quiet evening, shattering the tranquility of my surroundings. Daddy's voice trembled as he delivered the news, his words carrying a weight that seemed to press down on my chest.

"Lisa," he said, his voice barely above a whisper, "your mom... she's gone."

The world around me seemed to blur as I struggled to comprehend the magnitude of his words. It felt like it had come to a standstill, and the reality of the situation remained elusive, just beyond my grasp.

"No, that can't be true," I replied, trembling with disbelief and denial. "She can't be gone."

Though gentle yet unwavering, Daddy's words served as an anchor amidst the storm of emotions. "I know it's hard to accept, Lisa. But she's at peace now."

As the days turned into nights and the shock began to ebb, I grappled with a profound sense of loss. Memories of our conversations, the laughter we had shared, and the unbreakable bond that had defined our relationship surged to the forefront of my mind, a bittersweet reminder of the love that had once been.

Amid my grief, I embarked on a journey of self-discovery, propelled by the memories of my mother's unwavering love. The photographs we had taken and the letters we had exchanged became precious artifacts that held within them the essence of our connection.

"Lisa," Daddy said one day, his voice gentle yet firm, "your mother's love will always be a part of you. It's a flame that can never be extinguished."

I nodded, tears streaming down my cheeks. "I just wish I had more time with her."

Daddy wrapped his arms around me, offering a solace that transcended words. "She's with you, Lisa. In your heart and your memories."

And so, as I navigated the spectrum of emotions that defined my journey through grief – from anger to bargaining, sadness to acceptance – I began to understand that my mother's passing was not an end but a new beginning. Her legacy lived on within me, a strength guiding me through the challenges ahead.

As the days turned into weeks and the pain began to dull, I found solace in knowing that my mother's love was a beacon that would forever light my path. The journey of self-discovery ignited by her passing became a testament to the enduring power of love, a force that transcended even the boundaries of life and death.

And as I looked back at the photograph from Briggs Elementary, my younger self staring back at me with innocence and curiosity, I couldn't help but feel a sense of gratitude for the memories we had shared, the lessons we had learned, and the love that had woven itself into the very fabric of my existence.

The journey ahead was uncertain, marked by twists and turns I could not yet foresee. But armed with the legacy of my mother's unwavering love, I was determined to embrace whatever challenges and mysteries awaited, knowing that her spirit would forever be a guiding light, illuminating the way toward a destiny that was uniquely my own.

My encounter with mortality had cast a stark spotlight on the preciousness of life, transforming each passing moment into a tapestry of newfound significance. The fragility of existence, once an abstract concept, had become an undeniable truth that colored every facet of my reality.

"Lisa," my father said one evening, his voice carrying a soothing warmth, "life is a delicate dance of light and shadow. Even in the darkest moments, there's a glimmer of hope, a reminder that our loved ones live on within us."

His words resonated within me, a tribute to my mother's ethereal presence that seemed to linger in the air around us. The legacy of her love, the lessons she had imparted, and the moments we had shared, as few as they were, were all threads that wove together to form the tapestry of my existence.

As I navigated the intricate labyrinth of grief, I was drawn into a delicate dance between sorrow and gratitude. Like a heavy cloak, the pain of loss enveloped me in moments of introspection and vulnerability. Yet, within that pain existed a space for gratitude – a space where I could celebrate the moments we had shared, the love that had bound us, and the legacy that continued to shape my journey.

"Lisa," Mack said one afternoon, her eyes filled with compassion and understanding, "grief is a complex journey. It's okay to feel a spectrum of emotions."

I nodded, a silent acknowledgment of the truth in her words. "I'm learning that it's okay to mourn and simultaneously find joy in the memories."

Fayeola's smile was a beacon of reassurance. "Your journey is your own, Lisa. Embrace every emotion and let them guide you."

And so, within the delicate dance of grief and gratitude, I began to uncover a wellspring of strength I had never known existed. The legacy of my mother's love, the wisdom of my father's comforting words, and the bond that held our family together – became pillars of support as I navigated the complexities of life's tapestry.

As the days turned into months and the seasons cycled through their eternal dance, I embraced life's intricacies with a newfound sense of purpose. Each sunrise held the promise of a new beginning, each sunset a moment of reflection and gratitude. The moments of laughter shared with friends and the quiet conversations with loved ones became brushstrokes that painted a portrait of resilience and growth.

And so, as I looked back on the journey that had brought me to this point, I couldn't help but feel a profound sense of awe for the mysteries that had unfolded. The delicate dance of grief and gratitude had set the stage for a remarkable transformation. This transformation allowed me to embrace the complexities of life with open arms, find strength in the legacy that preceded me, and carry forward the flame of love that would forever light my path.

The road ahead remained uncertain, a continuation of the enigmatic journey that my mother's passing had ignited. But armed with the lessons of grief and gratitude and the echoes of her unwavering love in my heart, I was ready to face whatever challenges and mysteries lay ahead, knowing that her spirit would forever guide me through the labyrinth of life's intricate tapestry.

Chapter 5: Farewell to a Warrior

The journey began with a piggyback ride to the river, the voice of my daddy carrying the weight of a decision that held profound significance. "Lisa," Daddy said, his words measured and filled with a sense of purpose, "your mother is coming home."

The news hung in the air like a whispered prayer, a beacon of hope amidst the darkness of grief. The grace, orchestrated by Reed & Culver Funeral Home, embodied a daughter's love and a community's solidarity, a testament to the power of unity and compassion.

As the plane touched down on the familiar soil of Tahlequah, Indian Country, Oklahoma, I felt a mixture of emotions – sadness for the loss that had brought us here and gratitude for the opportunity to honor my mother's memory in a place that held such profound significance to her.

The streets of Tahlequah seemed to embrace us with open arms, a silent chorus of support and understanding that resonated with every step we took. The final journey from the airport to Reed & Culver Funeral Home was a pilgrimage that celebrated my mother's life, her legacy, and her unwavering spirit.

"Lisa," the funeral home director said, his eyes reflecting a deep sense of empathy, "we're here to ensure that your mother's final resting place is among the landscapes woven into the fabric of her identity."

Standing before my mother's casket, held in my daddy's arms, surrounded by loved ones and the collective embrace of a community, I couldn't help but feel a profound sense of closure. The journey had come full circle – from the whispers of the past to the present moment of farewell; every step had been guided by a love transcending time and space.

The ceremony was a symphony of emotions, a blend of tears and laughter that danced on the edge of remembrance. The eulogies and tributes painted a vivid portrait of my mother's indomitable spirit, her fierce determination, and the legacy she had left behind. The notes of her life story, woven with threads of love and resilience, resonated in the hearts of all who gathered to honor her memory.

As the sun set over Tahlequah, casting a golden hue over the landscape, we reached the final resting place – a serene corner of the earth that would cradle my mother's physical form while her spirit soared free. Laying her to rest was a profound expression of closure, a moment where grief and gratitude converged in a final farewell.

"Goodbye, Mom," I whispered, my voice carried by the wind that rustled through the trees. "Your journey has ended, but your legacy will forever live on."

As we left the cemetery, the echoes of the ceremony and the memories of my mother's life lingered like a whispered prayer. The journey had concluded, but the tapestry of her legacy continued to unfold, a testament to the enduring power of love, resilience, and the unbreakable bond that united us all.

And so, as we embarked on the road that would lead us away from Tahlequah, I carried with me the lessons of a life well-lived, the embrace of a community that had stood by our side, and the knowledge that my mother's spirit would forever guide me through the labyrinth of life's mysteries. The curtain had fallen on a warrior's journey, but the echoes of her strength and the imprint of her love would forever remain etched in the tapestry of our hearts.

As we bid farewell to my mother, Mary Ann Eslinger, her obituary became a vessel that encapsulated the very essence of a life that had burned brightly, leaving an indelible mark on the tapestry of existence. Born as "Sosti" Groundhog, her name held within it echoes her Cherokee heritage, a heritage that would shape her into a woman of unparalleled strength, resilience, and advocacy.

"Sosti," Fayeola said, her voice reverent as she shared stories of my mother's early years, "was a name that echoed through the generations, a name that carried the weight of our people's history and the legacy of our ancestors."

The words held a profound significance, each syllable a tribute to the roots firmly planted in the heart of Tahlequah. From the very beginning, my mother's journey was destined to be one that would echo through generations, leaving a trail of inspiration and empowerment that would transcend the boundaries of time.

The obituary painted a vivid portrait of my mother's life – a life marked by the fires of advocacy and the unyielding determination to bring about change. Her involvement in the American Indian Movement, her alliances with influential figures, including Ted Kennedy and Ronald Reagan, and her unwavering commitment to justice were the threads that wove together to form the rich tapestry of her legacy.

"Lisa," my father said, his eyes reflecting a mixture of pride and sorrow, "your mother's legacy is a testament to the power of standing up for what is right, even in the face of adversity."

I nodded, my heart swelling with reverence for the woman who had carved a path of courage and strength for herself and those who would follow. "She never backed down from a challenge and always fought for those who couldn't fight for themselves."

The obituary became a tribute to the warrior spirit that had defined my mother's existence. Her name, "Sosti," symbolized her connection to her heritage and her role as a fierce protector and advocate for her people. From the roots of her birth in Tahlequah, she had embarked on a journey that transcended the limitations of time, leaving a trail of words and actions that would resonate far beyond her years.

As I stood before the gathered community, my eyes scanning the faces of those who had come to pay their respects, I felt a profound gratitude. My mother's legacy was not only a reflection of her accomplishments but a reflection of our people's collective strength and resilience.

"Sosti Groundhog Eslinger," I said, carrying the weight of a daughter's love and a community's solidarity, "your journey has come full circle. Your legacy will forever burn brightly, guiding us through the challenges ahead."

And so, as we bid our final farewell to a warrior whose spirit had touched countless lives, I couldn't help but feel a sense of awe for the journey that had unfolded. From the heart of Tahlequah to the farthest reaches of advocacy, my mother's name had become synonymous with courage, determination, and a steadfast commitment to improving the world.

I carried with me the echoes of her strength, the imprints of her love, and the knowledge that her legacy would forever be a beacon of hope in a world that often seemed shrouded in darkness. The final curtain had fallen, but the echoes of her life's symphony would forever resonate in the hearts of those her presence had touched.

As the tapestry of my mother's life unfurled before us, her literary endeavors emerged as a testament to the depth of her character and the unwavering fire that burned within her. The words she penned, like whispered prayers carried on the wind, unveiled a woman of substance who used her voice to cast a searing light on the shadows of injustice.

"Sosti's words were like arrows that pierced the heart of exploitation," Fayeola said, her eyes reflecting pride and solemnity. "Through her writing, she brought to light the struggles faced by Native American girls – struggles that had remained hidden in the dark corners of society for far too long."

The titles of her works – "GI-Dee-Thlo-Ah-Ee of The Blue People Clan" and "Cherokee People" – held within them the power to ignite change and spark conversation. Through the pages of these literary creations, my mother had fearlessly exposed the dark underbelly of exploitation and human trafficking that had plagued our community, shedding light on a reality that demanded acknowledgment and action.

"Lisa," my father said, his voice steady and relentless, "your mother's writing was a call to arms, a clarion call for change reverberating through time."

I nodded, my heart swelling with a sense of awe for the woman who had harnessed the power of words to become a catalyst for transformation. "Her written words were a testament to her unwavering commitment to justice."

The pages of her books became a battlefield where she waged war against injustice, armed with the ink of her pen and the strength of her convictions. She refused to disregard the struggles faced by the most vulnerable members of our community, and through her writing, she rallied others to join her in the fight for a brighter, more just future.

"Sosti's words were a beacon of hope," Fayeola said, her voice filled with reverence. "She refused to let the voices of those who had been silenced go unheard."

The legacy of my mother's literary endeavors echoed through time, a chorus of voices that refused to be silenced. Her courage to tackle uncomfortable truths, dedication to shedding light on the darkest corners of society, and unyielding commitment to justice were the threads that wove together to form a tapestry of inspiration that would forever resonate with those who dared to listen.

As the ceremony honoring my mother's life concluded, I couldn't help but feel a profound gratitude for the woman who paved the way for a future filled with possibility. Her words, etched onto the pages of her books, were not only a testament to her strength but a testament to the collective strength of our community.

"Sosti Groundhog Eslinger," I whispered, my voice carried by a sense of reverence and determination, "your literary legacy will forever be a source of inspiration. Your words have the power to shape minds and ignite change."

And so, as we left behind the place where we had bid our final farewell to a warrior, I carried with me the echoes of her words, the imprints of her strength, and the knowledge that her legacy would forever be a guiding light in a world that yearned for transformation.

In the wake of my mother's passing, a new phase of her legacy began to unfold, a step that would be written through the life of her daughter – me, Lisa Christine Christiansen. The bond between mother and daughter, forged through love, courage, and shared struggles, became a bridge that spanned generations, connecting us in a tapestry of strength and resilience.

"Sosti's legacy lives on through you, Lisa," Fayeola said, her eyes filled with pride and tenderness. "Her spirit flows through your veins, a river of determination and empowerment."

The words held a weight that settled deep within my heart. My mother's story had become entwined with mine, a journey of discovery and empowerment guided by the echoes of her stubborn spirit.

As the sad clouds of grief loomed overhead, the Cedar Tree Baptist Church transformed into a sanctuary of remembrance, a sacred space where my mother's life was celebrated, and her journey was honored. The community gathered each face a reflection of the impact she had made, each heart a vessel of gratitude for the woman who had stood as a beacon of light against the currents of adversity.

The eulogies and tributes painted a vivid portrait of my mother's life – a portrait that mirrored the landscape of her homeland, rich with the colors of love, compassion, and unwavering strength. As I stood before the congregation, my voice steady and filled with reverence, I couldn't help but feel a profound sense of pride.

"My mother," I said, carrying the weight of a daughter's love and a warrior's respect, "was a force of nature, a woman who defied the odds and left a permanent mark on this world."

The church was filled with a chorus of nodding heads and murmurs of agreement, a testament to the truth in my words. My mother's legacy was empowerment and inspiration, a gift that had the power to spark change and ignite the flames of justice in the hearts of those who carried it forward.

As the ceremony drew close, my gaze shifted to the words etched in the pages of "Our People and Where They Rest" Vol 10, a testament to my mother's indelible mark on her homeland and the hearts of those who had known her. The echoes of her stubborn spirit found new life within me, inspiring my journey of discovery and empowerment.

"Sosti Groundhog Eslinger," I whispered, my voice carrying a sense of determination and gratitude, "your spirit lives on within me, a guiding light that will forever illuminate my path."

And so, as the congregation dispersed and the church emptied, I carried with me the echoes of my mother's life – a life marked by strength, resilience, and unwavering commitment to justice. The final farewell had been bid, but the legacy she had left behind would forever be a source of inspiration, a beacon of light that would guide me through the challenges and mysteries of life's intricate tapestry.

As the physical presence of my mother, Mary Ann Eslinger, faded into the realm of memory, her legacy blazed on with an intensity that seemed to defy the passage of time. Like an eternal flame, her influence cast a warm and unwavering light, illuminating the path of justice and empowerment for generations to come.

"Sosti's legacy lives on through you, Lisa," Fayeola said, her voice carrying a sense of reverence. "You are the torchbearer of her unwavering determination and boundless love."

Her words resonated deep within me, a reminder of the responsibility and honor of carrying forward my mother's legacy. The fiery determination that had characterized her life had become a torch that I now carried, a torch that would continue to shine brightly and inspire those who walked alongside me on this journey.

As the days turned into weeks and the seasons continued their eternal dance, I embraced my role as the torchbearer with purpose and resolve. My mother's legacy was not confined to the past; it was a living, breathing force that propelled me forward, guiding my actions and fueling my determination to make a difference.

"Lisa," my father said one evening, his eyes filled with pride and encouragement, "your mother's fire lives on within you. Let it guide you and light the way for others."

I nodded, affirming my commitment to honor my mother's memory by continuing her work. "I will carry her flame with pride, Dad."

In the legacy of words penned with purpose, actions driven by conviction, and a love that knew no bounds, my mother's story remained an unending source of inspiration. Her courage to stand against injustice, her commitment to lifting the voices of the marginalized, and her unwavering belief in the power of love and unity – were the pillars upon which her legacy stood.

"Sosti's legacy is a beacon of hope," Fayeola said, conveying certainty. "Her story will forever illuminate the path of justice, inspiring those who come after us."

And so, as I walked this path of empowerment and advocacy, I carried with me the echoes of my mother's life – echoes that served as a reminder of the strength that resided within me, a force that had been passed down through generations. The torch I held symbolized her legacy and a commitment to ensure that her fire continued to burn brightly, guiding others toward a future where justice, compassion, and love reign supreme.

"Sosti Groundhog Eslinger," I whispered, my voice filled with determination and gratitude, "your legacy will forever be a light source in a world that often needs guidance."

I embraced my role as the torchbearer, fueled by the fire of my mother's legacy. The final farewell had been bid, but the journey of empowerment and justice was far from over. With every step I took, every word I spoke, and every action I undertook, I knew that my mother's spirit walked beside me, an eternal presence that would forever illuminate the path ahead.

Chapter 6: A Shift in Perspective

The year was 1976, and the world around me seemed moving in a familiar and unfamiliar rhythm. Life continued its intricate dance of celebrations and hardships, weaving a tapestry of experiences that molded my journey in ways I couldn't have anticipated.

The unexpected union of my father and aunt, Mack and Fayeola, was a twist of fate I hadn't seen coming as they stood before Minister Kenneth Littledave, a sense of familial bond intertwined with a deeper, spiritual connection. Their eyes met, and it was as if the universe itself had orchestrated this union, guiding them toward a new phase in our collective journey.

"Dearly beloved," Minister Littledave began, his voice carrying a sense of solemnity and joy, "we are gathered here today to celebrate not only the union of two souls but the intertwining of two destinies."

As I stood there, a witness to this unexpected union, I couldn't help but feel a mixture of emotions – happiness for my father and aunt, curiosity about the path ahead, and a sense of awe at the mysterious ways life unfolds.

"Do you, Mack Vann, take Fayeola Spears to be your lawfully wedded wife?" Minister Littledave's question hung in the air, a pivotal moment that would shape the course of our family's journey.

"I do," my father said, his voice strong and unwavering.

"And do you, Fayeola Spears, take Mack Vann to be your lawfully wedded husband?"

"I do," my aunt responded with a sense of determination and playfulness.

As the ceremony continued, I couldn't help but reflect on the evolving landscape surrounding us. My perceptions were shifting, deepening in ways that allowed me to see beyond the surface and into the heart of socioeconomic disparities that had profound implications for families like ours.

The dance of celebrations and hardships took on new meaning as I witnessed the strength and resilience of my family. Our bond was a source of solace and support, a reminder that love and unity could carry us through even the most challenging times.

"Life is an interwoven mystery," my aunt said one evening, her eyes reflecting wisdom from lived experiences, "woven with threads of joy and sorrow, of triumphs and tribulations."

I nodded, absorbing her words like a sponge, eager to learn and grow. "But it's in those contrasts that we find the true essence of our journey, isn't it?"

She smiled a warm and knowing smile. "Indeed, Lisa. It's through the contrasts that we gain perspective that we learn to appreciate the beauty and complexity of life."

And so, as the year 1976 continued its dance, I embraced the shifting perspectives that came with each new experience. The unexpected union of my father and aunt marked a turning point. This moment deepened my understanding of the world and ignited a fire within me to stand against socioeconomic disparities and advocate for change.

As the days turned into weeks and the seasons changed, I walked a path illuminated by the flames of newfound awareness. The journey ahead was uncertain, but I was ready to face it head-on, armed with a shifted perspective and a determination to make a difference in a complex world full of potential.

At the tender age of 10, the curtain of innocence began to lift, revealing a world of stark contrasts that I had previously only glimpsed from the periphery. As I navigated this new phase of my journey, my perception of the world around me deepened, and I became acutely aware of the complexities beneath the surface.

During this time, I first encountered the concept of socioeconomic levels. The lines that divided people based on their circumstances became increasingly apparent, and I found myself straddling two distinct worlds – that of a Johnson O'Malley child and that of a recipient of Christian Children's Fund support.

My identity became a patchwork of experiences, a mosaic of privilege and struggle that shaped the lens through which I viewed the world. I became attuned to the disparities within our community and saw firsthand the impact that socioeconomic factors could have on individuals and families.

One evening, as the sun dipped below the sky and painted the sky with hues of gold and crimson, I found myself in a quiet moment with my father. The fire crackled softly, casting a warm glow on our faces as we sat beside it.

"Daddy," I began tentatively, "I've been thinking about the different things we have and the challenges some of our friends and neighbors face."

My father's gaze met mine, his eyes carrying wisdom from years of navigating the intricacies of life. "Life isn't always fair, Lisa. Some people are born into circumstances that make their journey more difficult."

I nodded, absorbing his words like a sponge. "But why, Dad? Why do some people have so much, and others have so little?"

He sighed, his expression a mixture of empathy and resolve. "It's a question that has troubled humanity for generations. But what matters is how we respond to these disparities. We must never forget our responsibility to help those in need."

As I grappled with these newfound insights, I witnessed my father's tireless efforts to provide for our family. His days were filled with hard work, often hunting for sustenance and working to ensure that we had enough to get by.

"Your father," my aunt said to me one day, her voice filled with pride, "is a symbol of resilience and determination.

He teaches us that no matter the circumstances, we have the power to overcome."

And overcome, he did. Through his actions, my father imparted valuable life lessons that would ultimately forge a foundation of empathy, gratitude, and resilience within me. I learned the importance of helping those in need, never taking blessings for granted, and finding strength in adversity.

As I navigated the intricate dance of life, I carried these lessons with me, a constant reminder of the power of compassion and the importance of standing up against injustice. The curtain of innocence had lifted, revealing a complex and multi-faceted world. Still, through these experiences, I began to understand the true essence of empathy and the transformative impact it could have on individuals and communities.

The year was 1976, and with each passing day, I continued to evolve, grow, and embrace the shifting perspectives that would shape my journey in ways I could have never imagined.

Among the formative moments that etched themselves into my memory, one transformative encounter remains vivid, a turning point that would forever shape my understanding of selflessness and the profound impact of giving beyond one's means.

It was a crisp autumn afternoon, and I stood before the Welling Store, a small commerce oasis nestled within our community's heart. The sun bathed everything in a warm, golden glow, and the air was tinged with the sweet scent of fallen leaves.

I watched as people bustled about, each absorbed in their world of errands and conversations. But my attention was drawn to a woman sitting on the store's steps, her weathered face a canvas of resilience and weariness.

I hesitated for a moment, a flurry of emotions swirling within me. On the one hand, there was a desire to indulge in a personal treat, a small luxury that would momentarily ease the complexities of life. On the other hand, there was a tug of empathy, a recognition of the woman's need that called upon my sense of compassion.

My father's wisdom echoed in my mind, his words a steady beacon of guidance. "Lisa," he had said, his voice a gentle reminder, "it's in our moments of choice that we reveal our true character."

I approached the woman with a deep breath and offered a warm smile. "Are you okay?"

She looked up, her eyes meeting mine, and a faint smile graced her lips. "Just a bit tired, dear."

At that moment, a decision was made, a seemingly simple choice that would carry weight far beyond its immediate impact. I reached into my pocket, pulled out a few coins – meager resources meant for something frivolous – and extended them towards her.

"Here," I said softly, "maybe this can help."

Her eyes widened, a mixture of surprise and gratitude dancing within them. "Thank you, child. Bless your kind heart."

As I watched her count the coins, a sense of warmth spread through my chest. But it wasn't until later that I would truly understand the significance of that moment – a significance that would unfold in the most unexpected and awe-inspiring way.

Days turned into weeks, and life continued its dance. But it was on one fateful evening, as the sun dipped below the horizon and painted the sky with orange and pink, that the ripple effect of that simple act of generosity would reveal itself.

A knock at our door interrupted the quiet of the evening. I opened it to find a gentleman looking for a farmhand, asking for my daddy to build a fence. My daddy accepted his offer, and I was to record his hours in a notebook. He returned with boxes filled with provisions – food, clothing, and essentials that were far beyond what my meager contribution could have provided.

"The kindness you showed has come full circle," the note read. "May this be a reminder that even the smallest acts of compassion can set off a chain reaction of providence?"

At that moment, I felt a profound sense of awe, a recognition of the divine manifestation of giving beyond one's means. The encounter at the Welling Store had ignited a spark of generosity that had set off a chain reaction, touching lives and culminating in a manifestation of providence that left me humbled and deeply grateful.

From that day forward, the lesson of selflessness and the power of giving beyond one's means were forever engrained in my heart. The encounter had been a defining juncture, a testament to the far-reaching impact of even the simplest acts of kindness. And as I stood there, enveloped by a sense of wonder, I knew that this lesson would guide me on my journey of empathy, gratitude, and resilience, forever reminding me of the immense power we all possess to make a difference in the lives of others.

Chapter 7: Dreams and Determination

Amid life's intricacies, some moments shimmered like gems – moments that held a special place in my heart, forever etching themselves into the tapestry of my journey. One such moment was a seemingly simple, idyllic vision of a butter and jelly sandwich made with my father's touch.

I stood at the worn wooden table in our humble kitchen, my eyes fixed on the ingredients before me – a slice of bread, a dollop of butter, and a smear of sweet jelly. It might have appeared ordinary to some, but to me, it was a canvas upon which dreams were painted.

My father's hands moved with a practiced grace, each motion deliberate and gentle. He spread the butter with care, ensuring every corner was covered. Then, he added a layer of jelly, his touch transforming the humble ingredients into a masterpiece of flavors and textures.

"Daddy," I said, my voice filled with curiosity and excitement, "why do you always care about even the simplest things?"

He looked at me, his eyes carrying a depth of wisdom acquired through a lifetime of experiences. "Because, Lisa, it's in the simple things that we find the potential for greatness."

As I took a bite of the sandwich, I closed my eyes, savoring the harmony of flavors that danced upon my taste buds. But beyond the like, there was a deeper resonance – a metaphor for my aspirations and dreams.

In those moments at the Welling Store, as I encountered the disparities of socioeconomic levels and learned the lessons of empathy and service, my father's teachings became the foundation upon which I built my beliefs. The core belief in the significance of the heart, the power of extending a helping hand, and the immeasurable impact of small acts of kindness – were the principles that guided my path.

"Dream big, Lisa," my father would say, his eyes filled with encouragement and pride, "but remember that the journey to achieving your dreams is just as important as the destination."

I nodded, absorbing his words like a sponge, determined to channel my aspirations into actions that would bring about positive change. The idyllic vision of that butter and jelly sandwich became a constant reminder of the potential within me – the potential to transform the ordinary into the extraordinary, the potential to make a difference in the lives of others.

As the days turned into weeks, I held onto those moments of clarity and inspiration. The lessons I had learned at the Welling Store had shaped my worldview, deepening my understanding of the world's complexities and igniting a fire within me to be a force for good.

 "Dreams are like seeds," my father said one evening, his voice carrying a sense of quiet determination, "and determination is the soil that helps them grow."

And so, armed with dreams and determination, I embarked on a journey that would take me to places I had never imagined. The lessons I had learned, the values I held dear, and the belief in the power of empathy and service – were the guiding stars that illuminated my path, propelling me forward as I worked to make my aspirations a reality.

At the age of 13, amid my humble surroundings, fate orchestrated a serendipitous encounter that would plant a seed of aspiration within me. It was a balmy summer evening when I stumbled upon a movie playing on television – "Corvette Summer." Little did I know that this seemingly ordinary moment would set the wheels of determination into motion.

I watched with wide-eyed wonder as the story unfolded on the screen – a tale of adventure, dreams, and a quest for something more. As I followed the characters' journey, a fire ignited within me – a determination to defy the odds and transcend the societal expectations that had bound me.

"Daddy," I said excitedly, rushing into the living room where he was reading a Bible written in Cherokee, "have you ever thought about dreams that are bigger than what we see around us?"

He looked up, a knowing smile gracing his lips. "Oh, plenty of times, Lisa. Dreams are like the stars – they shine even when the night is at its darkest."

Inspired by the movie and my father's words, a new phase in my journey began to unfold. I realized that the world was vast, full of possibilities beyond the confines of my immediate surroundings. And so, armed with an unwavering commitment to excellence and the pursuit of dreams, I set out to carve a path that would lead me beyond the ordinary bounds that society had set.

My determination became my driving force. I threw myself into my studies, fueled by the belief that education was the key to unlocking a future different from anything I had ever known. The hours I spent poring over books and delving into new subjects felt like steps toward a brighter tomorrow.

One evening, my father approached me as the sun dipped below the horizon, casting a warm glow over the landscape. "Lisa, I've been watching you," he said, his voice a mixture of pride and encouragement, "and I couldn't be more proud of the commitment you've shown."

I smiled, humbled by his words. "Daddy, I want to make a difference, to show that dreams can become a reality no matter where we start."

He nodded, his eyes reflecting a deep understanding. "Remember, it's not about where you start – it's about where you're determined to finish."

I kept that sentiment close to my heart. I worked tirelessly, fueled by the belief that I had the power to shape my destiny. Each achievement, each step forward, was a testament to the determination ignited within me.

Against my humble surroundings, I forged a path that was uniquely mine. I pursued higher education, challenging myself to excel and prove that dreams could become a reality. The seed of aspiration planted during that serendipitous encounter with "Corvette Summer" had grown into a mighty oak of determination, casting a shadow of possibility over everything I did.

"Dreams are the bridges that connect the present to the future," my father said one day, carrying the weight of wisdom and experience. "And determination is the force that helps us cross those bridges."

And so, armed with dreams and determination, I continued my journey – a journey that would take me beyond the ordinary bounds and into a life shaped by the power of aspiration. As the years unfolded, I looked back on that pivotal encounter with gratitude, recognizing that even the simplest moments could spark a fire that burned bright, illuminating a path that was mine to forge.

As the years rolled on, a profound realization began to dawn upon me – a realization that would forever alter the course of my life. I understood that circumstances need not confine life, that the confines of my humble surroundings were merely a starting point, not a destination.

One evening, I found myself gazing out at the sunset, the hues of orange and pink painting the sky with a breathtaking palette. The world felt vast, with opportunities beyond what I had ever imagined. And at that moment, I made a deliberate choice – to embrace ambition and foster personal growth, to believe in the power of my dreams to transcend any limitations.

"Daddy," I said softly, my voice carrying determination and hope, "I want to create a life different from what we've known. I want to make a mark, to show that our circumstances don't define us."

He turned to me, his eyes holding pride and support. "Lisa, you've always had the potential to do great things. Remember, your wings are meant for soaring, not staying grounded."

And with those words, the lessons from the Welling Store – the encounters, the conversations, the acts of kindness – became a touchstone for me. They constantly reminded me of the power of choice and the potential in every decision.

Armed with this newfound perspective, I embarked on a journey of personal growth. I pursued education and skill development opportunities, determined to acquire the tools I needed to carve my unique trajectory. The determination that fueled my studies now guided me as I sought new experiences, met new people, and ventured beyond the boundaries that had once felt confining.

As I walked through the halls of learning, I held onto the belief that my dreams were within reach and that my beginnings did not bind my ambitions. Each step forward felt like a declaration of intent, a statement to the universe that I was ready to transcend any obstacles.

"Daddy," I said one evening, reflecting on my journey, "do you remember those lessons from the Welling Store? They've become my guiding light."

He nodded, his eyes reflecting a sense of pride and nostalgia. "Lisa, those lessons were never meant to be confined to a store. They'll be carried with you, illuminating your path wherever you go."

And so, armed with the wisdom of the Welling Store and the unwavering belief in the power of decision, I carved a trajectory that was uniquely mine. The ambitions that had once seemed distant now felt tantalizingly close, and with each milestone I achieved, I felt the weight of possibility settling upon my shoulders.

"Dreams are the architects of our destiny," my father would often say, his voice a reminder of the potential within me. "And it's up to us to build the life we envision."

With dreams as my blueprint and determination as my foundation, I embarked on a journey that would take me beyond the ordinary, beyond the confines of circumstance, and into a life that reflected my aspirations. The realization that cases need not constrain life became my driving force, reshaping my worldview and propelling me toward a future defined by ambition, growth, and the unwavering belief in the power of my decisions.

With every step I took on my journey of growth and self-discovery, the lessons from the Welling Store were a steady compass, guiding me through uncharted territories. As I reached higher, pushed farther, and dared to dream bigger, I held the belief that the power to shape my destiny lay within my hands.

"Daddy," I said one evening, reflecting on how far I had come, "those moments at the Welling Store taught me that we can shape our paths, regardless of where we start."

He smiled, his eyes filled with a mixture of pride and contentment. "Lisa, you've embraced the spirit of those lessons and transformed them into a reality. Your journey is a testament to the power of choice and determination."

And so, as I stand here today, looking back on the path I've walked, I am grateful for the lessons that have shaped me. The realization that circumstances do not confine life has become my mantra, my driving force. The deliberate choice to embrace ambition, foster personal growth, and believe in the transformative power of my dreams has reshaped my worldview.

The lessons from the Welling Store have become a part of who I am – a touchstone that reminds me that every decision I make can lead me closer to my aspirations. As I journey forward, I am guided by the unwavering belief that the power of decision is a force to be reckoned with, capable of transcending any limitations.

"Dreams are the seeds of our future," my father's voice echoes in my mind, his words a constant reminder of the potential within me. "And with determination as your guide, you can watch them bloom."

And so, armed with dreams, determination, and the lessons from the Welling Store, I continue to carve my unique path. I dare to dream big, reach for the stars, and to shape a life that reflects my aspirations. With each step forward, I am reminded that life is a canvas waiting to be painted, a journey waiting to be written, and a legacy waiting to be left behind.

I carry the lessons of the past with me – the wisdom of the Welling Store, the belief in the power of choice, and the understanding that life is a tapestry woven with dreams and determination. And so, with a heart full of hope and a spirit fueled by the lessons I've learned, I embrace the future with open arms, ready to embrace whatever challenges and opportunities come my way, ready to continue shaping my destiny in the image of my dream.

Chapter 8: A Model's Odyssey

As I turned the page to a new phase, the universe's intricate design became more evident. It was a serendipitous encounter that would mark the beginning of an extraordinary journey that would take me into the captivating world of modeling.

"Lisa, have you ever thought about modeling?" The question came from a stand-in school photographer who saw something in me that I had never considered.

Modeling? The word carried an air of glamor and intrigue that I had only seen in magazines and on billboards. But me? A model? It felt like a distant fantasy.

As fate would have it, the photographer who took a picture of me was a freelance photographer for

Cosmopolitan and a staff photographer for Wilhelmina Models. The photo was taken during one of our school picture events. He saw something in that candid shot – a spark, a potential – and decided to reach out. "I think you have a unique look," he said, his voice blending enthusiasm and curiosity. "Would you be interested in doing a photoshoot?"

The idea both thrilled and intimidated me. The notion of stepping into a new world, of becoming a canvas upon which artistry could be painted, was exhilarating. And so, with excitement and nervousness, I agreed to give it a shot.

As the camera's lens focused on me, I felt a rush of emotions. I was no longer just Lisa, the girl from the small town. I was a canvas, a subject, a model. The experience was like stepping into a new identity, allowing me to explore a side of myself I had never known.

The local photo shoot turned into something more – an opportunity to collaborate with prominent names in the fashion industry. From Dillard's to Montgomery Wards, my journey in modeling was a whirlwind of photo shoots, runway shows, and the thrill of seeing my image grace the pages of magazines, including Vogue, Cosmopolitan, and Glamour, to name a few. Each step felt like a leap into the unknown, a dance between confidence and vulnerability.

"Daddy," I said one evening, my voice tinged with wonder, "can you believe this journey I'm on? It's like a dream."

He smiled, his eyes reflecting a sense of pride. "Lisa, you've always had a unique light about you. Modeling is just another way for that light to shine."

And shine it did. I felt a newfound empowerment with each photo shoot and runway walk. The world of modeling was a space where I could express myself, where my presence could convey stories, emotions, and concepts. It was a world where I could be more than just a face – a canvas, a storyteller, an inspiration.

As the camera's shutter clicked, freezing moments in time, I realized that modeling was not just about appearances; it was about evoking emotions, sparking conversations, and making an impact. It was a platform that allowed me to embrace my uniqueness, celebrate my individuality, and show that beauty came in all forms.

"Modeling is a journey," my friend, the photographer, told me one day, his words carrying a sense of wisdom. "And it's a journey that's uniquely yours."

And so, armed with the lessons of the Welling Store, the belief in the power of dreams, and the newfound confidence from my modeling journey, I stepped onto a path that was as exhilarating as it was unpredictable.

The realm of modeling had evolved into more than just a vocation for me. It had become a canvas upon which my ambitions, dreams, and aspirations were painted. With every step I took on the runway and every photo shoot that captured a fleeting moment, I was carving a path beyond the industry's confines.

"Lisa, you're a natural in front of the camera," a fellow model said one day as we prepared for a shoot. "It's like you were born for this."

The words resonated with me, reminding me how far I had come from the girl who once believed modeling was out of reach. As I saw my image grace the pages of magazines as I confidently walked the runway, I realized that this journey was not just about appearances—it was about embracing my uniqueness, celebrating my individuality, and inspiring others to do the same.

Through unforeseen twists and turns, my journey in modeling led me to places I had only dreamed of. The unexpected opportunity to grace the cover of Cosmopolitan magazine was a moment of surreal triumph. I stood before the camera, a tapestry of emotions weaving within me – excitement, gratitude, and a sense of accomplishment that seemed to stretch beyond the boundaries of the glossy page.

"Daddy," I said one evening, my voice filled with amazement, "I can't believe I'm on the cover of Cosmo. It's like a dream come true."

He smiled, his eyes reflecting a sense of pride and joy. "Lisa, your journey is a testament to your determination and the power of your dreams."

But the journey didn't stop there. Vogue and Cosmopolitan magazines also beckoned, welcoming me within their pages. It was a realization of aspirations that had once seemed out of reach, a testament to the belief that with dedication and perseverance, even the loftiest goals could become a reality.

I continued navigating the fashion world; the runway became more than just a platform for showcasing clothing. It became a stage to convey stories, inspire conversations, and challenge norms. Each walk down the runway felt like a dance between art and self-expression, a powerful reminder that beauty was not confined to a singular mold.

"Modeling is an art," a designer told me as I prepared for a runway show, his eyes gleaming excitedly. "And you're an artist, bringing life to each creation."

The sentiment resonated with me deeply. Modeling has become a conduit for my ambitions – a way to express myself, challenge perceptions, and inspire others to embrace their uniqueness.

With every step, every pose, and every photoshoot, I realized that my journey extended beyond the realm of fashion. Modeling was a stepping stone, a Launchpad for something greater – a more profound purpose that drove me to use my platform for positive change, to uplift voices that had been marginalized, and to break down the barriers that confined beauty to narrow definitions.

"Dreams have the power to shape realities," my father's words echoed in my mind, a constant reminder of the transformative potential within each aspiration.

And so, as I continued to walk the runway of life, I carried the lessons of the Welling Store, the belief in the power of dreams, and the conviction that beauty was not just skin deep. The journey had taken me to unimaginable heights. With each step forward, I was not just a model but an advocate for self-expression, diversity, and the celebration of individuality.

The runway's allure and the fashion world's glamor were undeniably captivating. However, as I stood amidst the flashing cameras and designer gowns, a burning desire for something more meaningful stirred. The applause and the camera flashes were brief, but my yearning for a lasting impact was timeless.

"Lisa, you're a natural in front of the camera," a fellow model said, echoing sentiments I had heard before. "But there's something about you that goes beyond just modeling."

Her words resonated deeply, a reminder that my journey had taken me to a crossroads where dreams and purpose intersected. The allure of modeling paled in comparison to my burning desire to make a meaningful impact, to create a legacy that would resonate for generations to come.

"Daddy," I shared one evening, my voice filled with a newfound determination, "I want my journey to go beyond the runway. I want to use this platform to make a difference."

He nodded, his eyes reflecting understanding and pride. "Lisa, you've always had a fire within you to make a positive impact. Your journey is just beginning."

As the fashion world continued to open its doors to me, I used each opportunity as a stepping stone for positive change. I collaborated with organizations that championed social causes, using my platform to shed light on issues that mattered deeply to me – from advocating for education and empowerment to raising awareness about social justice and equality.

"Modeling isn't just about looking beautiful," I shared during an interview, my voice resonating with passion. "It's about using our voices to amplify the voices of others, to bring attention to important issues."

The applause and recognition I received for my efforts were gratifying, but the impact – the real-world change – fueled my spirit. Seeing the faces of those whose lives were touched by our collective efforts and the awareness, we raised reminded me that my journey had transcended the superficial allure of the fashion world.

"Dreams are the catalysts for change," a fellow advocate told me one day, echoing the sentiment that had become a guiding force in my life. "And you're living proof of that."

With each step I took, with each cause I championed, I realized that my journey was a tapestry woven with purpose. The runway had been a launching pad, but the path beyond it genuinely defined my legacy. It was a legacy I hoped would inspire generations, a gift that showed the power of dreams, determination, and the unwavering commitment to creating a better world.

Standing at the precipice of uncharted territories, I knew that my journey was poised to venture into realms where dreams and purpose converged. The allure of the runway had led me here, but my burning desire for meaningful impact would carry me forward. And so, armed with the lessons of the Welling Store, the belief in the transformative power of dreams, and the conviction that purpose was the compass guiding my steps, I embraced the path ahead with open arms – ready to weave a legacy that would resonate far beyond the world of fashion, prepared to leave a mark that would illuminate the darkness, and ready to continue my odyssey towards a life of purpose, impact, and boundless potential.

The allure of the runway had carried me far, but my burning desire for a meaningful impact illuminated the path ahead. The applause and recognition were temporary, but the change I could bring about had the potential to leave a lasting mark on the world.

"Dreams without purpose are like stars without constellations," I mused one day, reflecting on my journey. "It's when we connect our dreams to a greater purpose that they truly shine."

As I continued navigating the fashion world, I embarked on initiatives beyond the spotlight. Collaborating with like-minded individuals and organizations, I lent my voice to causes that spoke to my heart, using the platform I had built to amplify the voices of those whose stories needed to be heard.

"Lisa, you're more than just a model," a colleague told me, his eyes reflecting admiration. "You're an advocate, a changemaker."

I was at a juncture where dreams and purpose were seamlessly woven together. The allure of the runway had given way to a calling that transcended appearances, a calling that propelled me to use my influence for the greater good.

"Daddy," I shared one evening, my voice filled with a sense of fulfillment, "I feel like I'm living a life of purpose."

He smiled, his eyes filled with a sense of pride that words couldn't express. "Lisa, your journey is an inspiration to us all."

And with those words, I realized that my journey was not just a personal odyssey but a journey that resonated with others who dared to dream beyond the ordinary. Each step I had taken, each decision I had made, had led me to this moment where dreams and determination had paved the way for an extraordinary life.

"A Model's Odyssey," I knew my journey was far from over. The runway had been a stepping stone, a launchpad for the boundless potential ahead. Armed with the lessons of the Welling Store, the belief in the power of dreams, and the unwavering determination to make a positive impact, I embraced the unknown with open arms.

With every stride, every word, and every endeavor, I would continue to weave my legacy – a legacy of dreams pursued, purposes fulfilled, and a life lived with intention. And as I ventured into the uncharted territories of my next phase, I carried the torch of change, knowing that the echoes of my journey would reverberate through the lives of future generations.

Chapter 9: Legacy of Greatness

As I stand here today, reflecting on the winding path that has brought me to this moment, a profound sense of gratitude envelops my journey. It's as if the universe had orchestrated each step, each twist and turn, leading me to where I am now. From the aspirations that bloomed at the Welling Store to the runways of the fashion world and beyond, the road I've traveled has been filled with surprises beyond my wildest imagination.

"Daddy," I confided one evening, a sense of wonder in my voice, "I can't believe how far I've come."

He smiled, his eyes reflecting a blend of pride and contentment. "Lisa, your journey is a testament to your resilience and determination."

"Lisa, your insights are invaluable," a colleague told me during a strategy meeting. "You have a unique perspective that brings fresh ideas to the table."

Those words reminded me that my journey had forged a unique blend of experiences, perspectives, and insights that I could contribute to the world around me. As I navigated the corridors of power and policy, I realized that my journey had prepared me for a role beyond what I had imagined.

Speaking at the White House, standing before a podium that had witnessed history, was a moment that left me humbled and amazed. My words carried the weight of the journey that had brought me here – a journey of dreams realized, challenges overcome, and a commitment to creating positive change.

"Daddy," I shared after the event, my heart still racing with the moment's thrill, "it's as if all those moments from the Welling Store were leading me here."

He nodded a glimmer of pride in his eyes. "Your journey has always been guided by purpose."

A new opportunity, a new challenge, I knew that my journey was poised for even greater heights. A historic campaign loomed on the horizon, a story that awaited its phase in the tapestry of my life.

"Dreams are the seeds of legacy," I mused one day, my voice filled with determination. "And I'm ready to sow them."

With each step I took and my decision, I carried the lessons of the past and the aspirations of the future. The legacy I aimed to leave behind was not just one of personal accomplishments but a legacy of greatness. This legacy inspired others to dream, overcome obstacles, and create positive change in their lives and the world.

I carried with me the belief that every dream, every aspiration, and every challenge was a stepping stone toward a legacy that would resonate through time. The road ahead held surprises and uncertainties, but I was ready to embrace them all – for I knew it was a testament to the power of dreams, determination, and the unwavering commitment to greatness.

And so, with the echoes of the Welling Store guiding my steps and the lessons of the past propelling me forward, I embarked on the next phase of my odyssey, ready to leave a legacy that would inspire generations to come.

I reflect on the journey that has brought me to this juncture; I'm reminded of the weight of ancestral greatness that bears upon me. The legacy of Sequoyah, my great-great-great-great-great grandfather, is a testament to the power of determination and vision. His creation of the Cherokee syllabary, a gift to our people, provided a means to communicate our stories, preserve our heritage, and forge a better future.

"Daddy," I shared with awe and humility, "Sequoyah's legacy is something I carry daily."

He nodded, a knowing smile on his lips. "Lisa, you come from a lineage of visionaries. Your journey is an extension of that legacy."

Despite all odds, Sequoyah's determination to create the Cherokee syllabary left an indelible mark on our history. He believed in the power of education and preserving our language and culture. His actions weren't just about his time; they were about shaping the future for future generations.

In many ways, his vision and commitment resonated with my journey. The runway, the world of fashion, the corridors of power – they all converged to form a narrative that aimed to create positive change and leave an enduring legacy.

"The syllabary was a way for our people to communicate and tell their stories," I said during a conversation with a group of young activists. "And now, it's up to us to continue that tradition."

Sequoyah's legacy was a beacon, guiding me as I navigated the complexities of my journey. The echoes of his determination fueled my pursuit of greatness – a greatness that was not just for myself but for the betterment of my community, my country, and the world.

I looked ahead to the historic campaign that awaited; I knew it was more than a personal endeavor. It was a continuation of a legacy handed down through generations that demanded courage, determination, and an unwavering commitment to shaping a better future.

"Daddy," I confided one evening, a sense of purpose in my voice, "I'm ready to continue Sequoyah's legacy."

He smiled, his eyes reflecting a pride that words couldn't capture. "Sequoyah's legacy lives on through you, baby girl."

And so, with Sequoyah's vision as my guide, I embarked on the next phase of my journey – a phase that could potentially leave an indelible mark on future generations. The runway, the White House, the pursuit of greatness – they were all part of a larger narrative that aimed to create positive change and forge a better future.

I stood at the intersection of my lineage and aspirations; I carried with me the weight of ancestral greatness. Sequoyah's legacy was a reminder that vision, determination, and the belief in a better tomorrow were the ingredients of an enduring impact.

And so, armed with the legacy of Sequoyah and the lessons of my journey, I embraced the road ahead with open arms. The story was far from over; it was just beginning. The pages of my life were waiting to be written, and I was ready to continue the legacy of greatness entrusted to me. This legacy would illuminate the path for generations, just as Sequoyah's vision illuminated mine.

Sequoyah's visionary work in crafting the Cherokee syllabary serves as a bridge that spans the gap between history and modernity. His legacy is not just a relic of the past but a living testament to his determination and impact on cultural continuity. As I reflect on his contributions, I'm reminded that his vision granted our people a voice that resonates across generations.

"Daddy," I remarked one day, my voice filled with admiration, "Sequoyah's legacy is a beacon of resilience."

He nodded, a sense of reverence in his gaze. "He believed in the power of education and communication. His work was a gift to our people."

Sequoyah's creation of the Cherokee syllabary was more than just a practical tool – it was a profound statement about preserving our heritage and language. The syllabary became a vessel for our stories, wisdom, and identity. His vision paved the way for cultural preservation, and his legacy lives on through the generations that continue to speak our native tongue.

During a gathering of tribal leaders, I shared my thoughts on Sequoyah's enduring legacy. "The syllabary is not just letters and symbols," I emphasized. "It's a testament to the resilience of our people and their commitment to keeping our traditions alive."

In many ways, my journey echoed the essence of Sequoyah's work. The runway, the White House, my advocacy – they were all extensions of his legacy, testaments to the power of determination and its impact on the world.

"Daddy," I confided, a sense of purpose in my tone, "I want to ensure that Sequoyah's legacy lives on through my actions."

He smiled, his eyes reflecting a sense of affirmation. "Your journey is a continuation of his legacy. Each step you take is a testament to his vision."

As I looked ahead to the next phase of my odyssey, I knew that pursuing greatness was not just a personal endeavor but a continuation of Sequoyah's legacy. The runway, the White House, the campaign – they were all interconnected threads in the tapestry of his vision.

With each stride, each decision, and each endeavor, I aimed to honor the legacy of Sequoyah. His work was a reminder that one individual's determination could spark a revolution of cultural continuity and resilience. And as I embraced the road ahead, I carried with me the belief that his legacy and my journey were intertwined – a gift that would continue to shape the narrative of greatness for generations to come.

The legacy of Sequoyah, my great-great-great-great-great-grandfather, continues to inspire my journey. His visionary work in crafting the Cherokee syllabary bridges the rich history of our people with the modern world. Through his determination, he granted us a voice that spans generations and resonates with our community's wisdom, stories, and identity.

"Daddy," I shared one evening, a sense of reverence in my voice, "Sequoyah's impact on our culture is immeasurable."

He nodded, his gaze filled with understanding. "His legacy lives on through our language and heritage."

Sequoyah's perseverance and commitment to education were not just historical footnotes but principles that continued to guide my journey. The syllabary is a testament to his belief in the power of communication and the importance of preserving our traditions.

As I spoke to a group of young Cherokee students, I emphasized the significance of Sequoyah's legacy. "He believed that our language was worth preserving. And now, it's up to us to carry that torch."

My journey, from the fashion runways to the halls of power, was a testament to the enduring impact of Sequoyah's legacy. Just as he bridged history with modernity, I aimed to bridge the gap between dreams and reality, between ambition and positive change.

"Daddy," I confided, a sense of purpose in my voice, "Sequoyah's legacy compels me to strive for greatness."

He smiled, his eyes reflecting a sense of pride. "You're continuing a legacy of determination and vision."

And so, as I stand at the intersection of the past and the future, I carry the weight of Sequoyah's legacy. His work was not just a contribution to history; it was a gift to our people, a beacon of resilience that continues illuminating our path.

As I look ahead to the upcoming campaign, I know my journey is not just about personal accomplishments but about creating positive change for the Cherokee People and beyond. The runway, the White House, and the legacy of Sequoyah are all threads that weave together the narrative of my life.

With each step and endeavor I pursue, I am reminded that Sequoyah's legacy lives on through me. His determination, vision, and unwavering belief in a better future serve as a guiding light as I strive for greatness.

And so, armed with the lessons of the past and the future aspirations, I embark on the next phase of my journey. The legacy of Sequoyah and the legacy I aim to create are intertwined – a legacy of greatness that will inspire generations to come, just as his legacy has inspired mine.

Chapter 10: An Extraordinary Grandfather

As the granddaughter of George Washington Groundhog, a profound sense of humility and gratitude courses through me. The honor of being connected to a man of extraordinary character and contribution is both humbling and awe-inspiring. His role as one of the last surviving code talkers is a testament to his bravery and impact on history.

"Daddy," I mused during a conversation, "Grandpa George's legacy is one of courage and heroism."

He nodded a glint of pride in his eyes. "He was a true hero, not only for our family but for our nation."

My grandfather's legacy, a code talker during World War II, was a beacon of inspiration that guided my journey. His ability to use our native language as a secret code played a pivotal role in ensuring the safety of our troops. His journey was marked by courage and sacrifice, qualities that shaped not only his life but the lives of countless others.

As I shared his story with young members of the Cherokee community, their eyes lit up with awe. "Your grandfather's contribution saved lives," I emphasized. "And his legacy lives on through the impact he made."

The resonance of his journey stretched far beyond our family, echoing through history as a symbol of determination and patriotism. His ability to overcome adversity and use his linguistic skills for the greater good was a lesson that transcended generations.

"Daddy," I confessed, a sense of determination in my voice, "Grandpa George's legacy fuels my aspirations."

He smiled, a knowing look in his eyes. "He would be proud to see the path you've carved."

As I looked ahead to the future, I knew that my journey was intertwined with my grandfather's legacy. The runway, the advocacy, and the pursuit of greatness found their roots in the lessons he taught through his actions.

With each step I took, I carried the weight of his legacy, symbolizing resilience, courage, and the power of using one's talents for a higher purpose. Just as he served his nation with honor, I aimed to help my community and the world with the same spirit of dedication.

And so, as I continued down the path he paved, I knew that his legacy would forever be a guiding light. His remarkable journey as a code talker served as a reminder that ordinary individuals can achieve extraordinary feats when driven by purpose and determination.

As I looked at the pages of his story and my own, I saw the threads of courage and inspiration that connected us. The legacy of George Washington Groundhog was a beacon that illuminated the way for generations to come, a gift I carried with me as I embraced the challenges and opportunities ahead.

I delved deeper into the moments of my grandfather's life; his heroism emerged as a shining beacon. George Washington Groundhog's indomitable spirit propelled him through combat alongside General George S. Patton, etching his name in the annals of history. His story was not just one of bravery but a narrative of dedication, sacrifice, and unwavering commitment.

"Daddy," I marveled, my voice tinged with admiration, "Grandpa George's journey reads like a testament to courage."

He nodded, a sense of pride evident in his expression. "He faced unimaginable challenges and overcame them with determination."

My grandfather's role as a code talker during World War II was only a fraction of the remarkable story that defined his life. His combat experiences, fighting alongside General George S. Patton's forces, showcased his unwavering dedication to his duty and fellow soldiers.

I shared his story with a group of young students, their eyes wide with fascination. "Your grandfather's bravery was extraordinary," I emphasized. "He risked his life to ensure the safety of his comrades."

The decorations he received, including Purple Hearts and Bronze Star Medals, were not just symbols of his courage; they were reminders of his sacrifices for his country. His courage was a beacon that guided him through the darkest of times and inspired those around him.

"Daddy," I confided, a sense of determination in my voice, "Grandpa George's heroism propels me forward."

He smiled, a knowing look in his eyes. "His legacy lives on through your actions and advocacy."

As I looked ahead to the future, I knew that my journey was intertwined with my grandfather's legacy. The runway, the advocacy, and the pursuit of meaningful impact were all extensions of the lessons he taught through his actions.

With each step I took and endeavor I pursued, I carried the weight of his legacy with me. The gift of George Washington Groundhog was not just a phase in our family history but a narrative that resonated with courage, dedication, and a deep sense of duty.

And so, as I continued on my path, I aimed to honor his legacy by embodying those same values. Just as he fought for his country, I sought to fight for justice, empowerment, and positive change for our community and the world.

As I looked at the pages of his story and my own, I saw the thread of heroism that connected us. The legacy of George Washington Groundhog was a guiding light that illuminated the way for generations to come, a gift that inspired me to rise to the challenges of my time.

And as I embraced the opportunities and responsibilities that lay ahead, I carried with me the belief that his legacy was not just a memory but a force that continued to shape the trajectory of my journey.

The tapestry of my grandfather's life extended far beyond the battlefield, weaving a legacy that touched the heart of Cherokee identity itself. As the Original Cherokee Community Organization (OCCO) founder, he passionately advocated preserving Cherokee traditions, language, and culture. His leadership demonstrated his unwavering commitment to these values, leaving an indelible mark on our community.

"Daddy," I remarked, a sense of awe in my voice, "Grandpa George's dedication to our Cherokee heritage was remarkable."

He nodded, his expression a mix of pride and reverence. "He believed in the importance of passing down our cultural legacy to future generations."

My grandfather's contributions to preserving Cherokee traditions were both profound and far-reaching. His role in the "Fight That Influenced Five Nations" showcased his commitment to upholding our culture's integrity, even in the face of challenges.

As I shared his story with fellow Cherokee community members, their admiration was palpable. "Your grandfather's work echoes through the generations," I emphasized. "He fought not just on the battlefield but for our cultural identity."

The impact of OCCO, founded by my grandfather, reverberated through our community. His dedication to our traditions, language, and customs laid the groundwork for a stronger sense of identity and unity among our people.

"Daddy," I confessed, my voice unwavering, "Grandpa George's legacy is impressive and drives me to continue his work."

He smiled, a knowing look in his eyes. "He would be proud to see the torch being carried forward."

As I looked ahead to the future, I recognized that my journey was deeply intertwined with my grandfather's legacy. Just as he fought to preserve our cultural heritage, I aimed to continue that fight through my advocacy and efforts.

With each step I took and endeavor I pursued, I carried the weight of his legacy with me. The gift of George Washington Groundhog was not just a phase in our family history but a narrative that resonated with cultural pride, unity, and the determination to safeguard our traditions.

And so, as I continued down my path, I aimed to honor his legacy by actively working to protect and celebrate our Cherokee identity. Just as he stood up for our community, I sought to stand up for justice, representation, and the preservation of our cultural legacy.

As I looked at the pages of his story and my own, I saw the thread of cultural stewardship that connected us. The legacy of George Washington Groundhog was a guiding light that illuminated the way for generations to come. This gift fueled my passion to continue his work and build upon his foundation.

And as I embraced the responsibilities and opportunities that lay ahead, I carried with me the conviction that his legacy was not just a memory but a force that continued to shape the trajectory of my journey and our shared mission.

Beyond the battlefield, my grandfather's leadership extended to the heart of Cherokee identity. As the Original Cherokee Community Organization (OCCO) founder, he tirelessly advocated for preserving our traditions, language, and culture. His dedication to these values was a passing sentiment and a lifelong commitment that impacted our community indelibly.

"Daddy," I reflected, a sense of reverence in my tone, "Grandpa George's legacy is a testament to his love for our Cherokee heritage."

He nodded, his eyes reflecting a mixture of pride and nostalgia as he told stories of days long gone, a simple era when he was trying to earn my Grandpa's approval to date my mother. "He believed that our cultural identity was something worth fighting for."

My grandfather's role in the "Fight That Influenced Five Nations" further exemplified his unwavering commitment to our cultural legacy. Through his advocacy, he demonstrated that preserving our traditions was not just a duty but a responsibility that required dedication and courage.

Sharing my grandfather's story with fellow Cherokee members, I could see the admiration in their eyes. "Your grandfather's work laid the foundation for our cultural resilience," I emphasized. "He understood that our identity should be celebrated and protected."

The impact of OCCO, driven by my grandfather's vision, was profound. His efforts paved the way for a stronger connection to our heritage, uniting our community in the face of change and adversity.

"Daddy," I admitted, a sense of purpose in my words, "Grandpa George's legacy motivates me to continue his mission."

He smiled, a knowing expression on his face. "He would be proud to see his legacy thriving."

Looking forward, I recognized that my journey was intrinsically tied to my grandfather's legacy. As he fought to preserve our culture, I aimed to carry that torch forward by advocating for cultural awareness, representation, and empowerment.

With each step I took and the initiative I pursued, I carried the weight of his legacy with me. The gift of George Washington Groundhog was not just a phase in our family history; it was a narrative of cultural pride, resilience, and the unwavering commitment to safeguarding our traditions.

As I turned the pages of his story and my own, I saw the thread of cultural stewardship that bound us together. The legacy of George Washington Groundhog was a guiding light that illuminated the path for generations to come. This gift fueled my determination to continue his work and elevate the voices of our community.

And as I embraced the challenges and opportunities that lay ahead, I carried with me the certainty that his legacy was not simply a memory but a force that continued to shape the course of my journey and our collective pursuit of preserving our cultural heritage.

Chapter 11: Defining Moments

The clash of perspectives between my grandfather George Washington Groundhog and W.W. Keeler was a defining moment in Cherokee history. This moment would shape the course of our community's identity and legacy. The collision of two contrasting visions revealed the complexity of our past and the challenges of charting a path forward.

"Daddy," I inquired, curiosity evident in my voice, "Tell me more about the clash between Grandpa George and W.W. Keeler."

He took a deep breath, his expression a mixture of contemplation and recollection. "It was a clash of ideologies," he began, "reflecting the struggle for defining the direction our Cherokee identity should take."

Keeler, a prominent figure in Cherokee leadership at the time, championed an approach that emphasized economic progress and assimilation into mainstream society. He believed that economic development would secure our people's future and bring prosperity to our community.

On the other hand, my grandfather, George Washington Groundhog, held steadfast to a community-based approach that highlighted the importance of preserving our traditions, language, and cultural identity. He understood that our strength lay in our connection to our roots and our commitment to passing down our heritage to future generations.

The tension between these two visions arose during a significant dispute with far-reaching implications. The clash wasn't just about differing viewpoints but about the essence of our Cherokee identity.

"Daddy," I questioned, a sense of gravity in my words, "How did this clash impact the Cherokee community?"

He sighed, his expression carrying the weight of history. "It led to divisions within our community," he explained. "Some saw Keeler's vision as a way to secure our future, while others aligned with Groundhog's belief in safeguarding our cultural heritage."

The clash between these ideologies took time to resolve. It sparked debates, discussions, and disagreements that echoed throughout our community. The choice between economic progress and cultural preservation became a defining crossroads that required us to confront the complexities of our identity.

The clash between George Washington Groundhog and W.W. Keeler was more than a mere dispute; it was a reckoning that forced us to confront questions about who we are, what we value, and how we envision our collective future. It was a moment that underscored the importance of balancing progress and tradition, economic growth, and cultural preservation.

Looking back, I understand that this clash was a pivotal phase in our history that shaped our community's identity trajectory. It was a phase that reminded us that our journey as Cherokee people is marked by the complexities of navigating change while holding onto the threads of our heritage.

And as I carried forward the legacy of George Washington Groundhog, I recognized the significance of honoring economic progress and cultural preservation. Their clash of perspectives wasn't just a dispute; it was a catalyst for self-reflection, a reminder that the course we chart is a delicate balance between the lessons of our past and the aspirations for our future.

Keeler's vision of a modernized Cherokee identity, rooted in economic growth and integration into the larger American economy, stood in stark contrast to Groundhog's unwavering commitment to preserving the core values of the Cherokee people. Their differing philosophies painted a vivid picture of the complexities of identity in a rapidly changing world, highlighting the intricate balance between tradition and progress.

"Daddy," I mused, a sense of intrigue in my voice, "The clash between Keeler and Groundhog seems like a clash between two fundamental principles."

He nodded, a knowing smile tugging at the corners of his lips. "It was indeed a clash that encapsulated the struggle between embracing the future and honoring our past."

Keeler's perspective, often aligned with assimilation, advocated for the Cherokee people to adapt to the dominant culture's ways. He believed economic progress and participation in the broader American society were the key to securing our community's future. In his eyes, the path to success required shedding certain aspects of our traditional identity.

On the other hand, my grandfather, George Washington Groundhog, held steadfast to the belief that our strength lay in our connection to our cultural heritage. He considered preserving our traditions, language, and way of life paramount. To him, economic progress should not come at the expense of sacrificing our identity and values.

As I explored the clash between these two influential figures, I realized that their differing perspectives spoke to a larger struggle many indigenous communities worldwide face. The tension between embracing change and preserving cultural identity was not unique to the Cherokee people; it was a universal challenge that resonated deeply.

"Daddy," I questioned, "how did this clash impact the Cherokee community on a broader scale?"

He leaned back. His eyes focused on the horizon as if retracing the steps of history. "It created divisions," he answered. "It prompted introspection about what it meant to be Cherokee in a rapidly evolving world."

The clash between Keeler and Groundhog wasn't just about policy differences but a fundamental question of identity. It forced the Cherokee community to define who they were in the face of changing times. It was a challenge that touched the very core of our cultural identity.

As I delved into history, I recognized that the clash between these two visions didn't result in a clear victory for either side. Instead, it left a legacy of complex discussions, ongoing debates, and continuous exploration of what it means to be Cherokee in the modern era.

The clash between Keeler and Groundhog taught me that our identity is a living, breathing entity that evolves with each generation. It reminded me that embracing progress doesn't have to mean forsaking our traditions and preserving our heritage doesn't have to hinder our growth.

Their clash wasn't just a historical moment but a reflection of the ongoing narrative shaping our community's journey. It reminded us that our identity is a tapestry woven with threads of tradition, progress, and the intricate dance between the two.

And as I carried their legacy forward, I understood that their clash wasn't a black-and-white scenario but a nuanced exploration of the many shades that color our identity as Cherokee people. It was a testament to the resilience of our community, the richness of our heritage, and the ongoing quest to find harmony between the old and the new.

Your grandfather George Washington Groundhog's steadfast commitment to safeguarding Cherokee heritage and language serves as an unwavering beacon of dedication. In the recesses of history, his firm stance against the forces that sought to dilute Cherokee identity stands as a testament to the power of conviction. As I journey deeper into the tapestry of his life, I uncover the layers of his leadership that continue to inspire and shape the spirit of the Cherokee people.

"Daddy," I inquired, a sense of admiration evident in my voice, "how did Grandpa George manage to stand so firmly against those challenges?"

He leaned forward, his eyes gleaming with pride. "It wasn't easy," he began, "but he believed that our heritage and language were the essence of who we are as

Cherokee people. He saw them as our link to the past and the foundation for our future."

I discovered that my grandfather's dedication wasn't just an abstract concept. He actively worked to preserve Cherokee traditions, advocating for the continuity of our way of life. He understood that our heritage was not just a relic of the past but a living entity that shaped our present and guided our future.

"Tell me more about his leadership," I urged, eager to uncover the details of his impactful journey.

My father's eyes lit up, a fond smile gracing his face. "He was a trailblazer advocating for Cherokee language education," he shared. "He believed that preserving our language was key to preserving our identity."

As I listened, I marveled at my grandfather's foresight. He recognized that language was more than just a means of communication; it was a vessel that carried the essence of our culture, traditions, and stories. Through his efforts, he paved the way for generations to continue speaking the language of our ancestors, ensuring that their wisdom and knowledge would be passed down.

"He also founded the Original Cherokee Community Organization," my father continued, "a platform dedicated to preserving our traditions and cultural practices."

The organization, OCCO, became a haven for those who shared my grandfather's vision. It was a place where community, tradition, and identity values converged, serving as a source of inspiration and strength for Cherokee people facing the challenges of a changing world.

As I immersed myself in my grandfather's leadership stories, I understood that his dedication was a solitary effort and a collective journey. He brought together individuals who shared his passion, united by a common goal of preserving our heritage.

His legacy goes beyond mere accomplishments; it's a legacy of spirit, determination, and the belief that our identity as Cherokee people is worth fighting for. He stood as a living testament that our traditions and values are worth protecting, even facing challenges.

And as I walked in his footsteps, I felt a renewed sense of purpose. His legacy reminds me that preserving our heritage and language is not just a duty; it's a privilege.

It's a way of honoring those who came before us and paving the way for those who will come after us.

The clash between Keeler and Groundhog was more than a momentary dispute; it was a mirror reflecting the intricacies of our identity. Through their conflict, the Cherokee people were challenged to define who they were and who they wanted to be. My grandfather's leadership in preserving our heritage offers a powerful answer to that question—a resounding declaration that our identity is worth cherishing, protecting, and passing on to future generations.

The dynamic between George Washington Groundhog and W.W. Keeler reverberates as a pivotal juncture in Cherokee history, a clash of visions that would leave an indelible mark on the trajectory of our people. The conflict between Keeler's modernized perspective and Groundhog's deep-seated commitment to heritage offers a window into the complex interplay of tradition and progress within a rapidly changing world.

"Lisa," my father said, his voice tinged with admiration and reflection, "it was a clash of ideals that represented the heart of our identity."

I leaned in, eager to absorb every detail. "What ideals were they representing?" I asked, my curiosity piqued.

My father took a moment to gather his thoughts, then began, "Keeler's vision was rooted in economic growth and integration into the broader American society. He believed the Cherokee people could secure a brighter future by embracing modernity and participating in the American economy."

I nodded, understanding the allure of progress and the promise of economic stability. It was a sentiment that resonated with the times, a way to ensure a better life for our people.

"But Groundhog," my father continued, "he saw our heritage, language, and traditions as the cornerstones of our identity. To him, preserving our culture wasn't just a matter of pride—it was a matter of survival."

I was captivated by the depth of their differing perspectives. On the one hand, the allure of modernity and economic prosperity; on the other, the steadfast commitment to the values that had sustained our people for generations.

"It wasn't just about their personal beliefs, Lisa," my father explained. "It was about what those beliefs represented for the Cherokee people as a whole."

I realized that this clash of visions wasn't merely a philosophical debate; it was a struggle for the very soul of our nation. Groundhog's steadfastness in the face of challenges symbolized resistance to cultural assimilation and a fight to preserve our unique identity.

"In a way," my father mused, "their clash encapsulated the struggle that many indigenous communities face— how to navigate the pressures of a changing world without compromising our heritage."

The tension between Keeler and Groundhog was a microcosm of the more significant battle in our hearts and communities. It forced us to question what it meant to be Cherokee in an evolving landscape.

Reflecting on their clash, I realized that both perspectives carried weight and importance. Keeler's vision represented a practical path to prosperity, while Groundhog's steadfastness reminded us that our heritage was the bedrock of our existence.

Their clash wasn't a simple black-and-white struggle; it was a tapestry woven with shades of gray. It reminded us that our choices as a community and individuals are never easy and that our decisions have far-reaching implications.

As I continued to uncover the layers of this defining moment, I felt a renewed sense of appreciation for the complexities of our history. The clash between Keeler and Groundhog wasn't just a dispute; it reflected the intricate dance between tradition and progress that shaped the Cherokee people.

Their clash didn't offer a clear answer—it offered a question. A question that continues to echo through time, challenging us to navigate the delicate balance between our heritage and the ever-changing world around us.

And as I looked to the future, I knew that their clash would forever guide us in defining our identity as Cherokee people—a pursuit that honors our past, embraces our present, and paves the way for future generations.

Chapter 12: Keeler's Contributions to the Bill and OCCO's Dissent

In the annals of Cherokee history, the legacy of W.W. Keeler takes center stage—a figure whose contributions and decisions would leave an indelible mark on our journey. As I delved deeper into the narrative, I encountered a defining moment that showcased his pragmatic approach and ignited dissent within the Original Cherokee Community Organization (OCCO).

I was transported to a pivotal meeting, where Keeler's proposal stirred interest and controversy among the community members. The atmosphere was charged with anticipation as Keeler stepped forward, his presence commanding attention.

"I propose that we consider using the term 'select' instead of 'elect' when it comes to choosing our tribal leaders," Keeler's voice resonated through the room, his tone measured yet resolute.

The room buzzed with a mixture of curiosity and skepticism. The proposal could impact the essence of our governance—a decision not to be taken lightly.

One of the older members of OCCO raised a hand, his voice carrying the weight of experience. "Mr. Keeler, could you elaborate on the reasoning behind this proposal?"

Keeler nodded, acknowledging the question. "Certainly. The idea stems from consideration for cost savings and efficiency. Our tribe is growing, and the process of elections requires significant resources. Instead of opting for a selection process, we can channel those resources into programs that benefit the community."

His explanation resonated with practicality, reflecting his dedication to the well-being of the Cherokee people.

Another member chimed in, her tone cautious. "But doesn't 'selection' imply a top-down approach? How do we ensure that the voices of our people are heard?"

Keeler's response was measured, his gaze steady. "I understand your concern. That's why any selection process would be designed to include community input. We could establish committees representative of various sectors, who would then contribute to the decision-making process."

The room seemed divided, caught between the desire for efficiency and the value of democratic representation. It was a clash of ideals, much like the clash between Keeler and Groundhog, with different interpretations of what was best for our community.

As I listened to the dialogues unfold, I couldn't help but be reminded of the complexities of leadership and decision-making. Keeler's proposal wasn't just about semantics; it reflected his approach to governance, which sought to balance practicality with community involvement.

But within the walls of OCCO, dissent was brewing. A young woman, her eyes alight with passion, raised her voice. "Mr. Keeler, while I understand the need for efficiency, our tradition of electing leaders is a cornerstone of our democracy. It ensures that the will of the people is upheld."

Keeler's response was respectful, a testament to his willingness to engage in dialogue. "Your perspective is valid, and I appreciate your commitment to our democratic process. I intend not to undermine that tradition but to explore ways to make it more effective."

We had a discussion that showcased the varied perspectives present in our community. It was a reminder that every decision—no matter how seemingly small—has far-reaching implications.

I reflected on Keeler's proposal and the dissent it had ignited. It was a vivid demonstration of the complexities that arise when attempting to balance progress with tradition, pragmatism with democratic values.

Keeler's legacy was marked not only by his contributions but also by the dialogues he sparked, the conversations that forced us to examine our values and aspirations. In that room, on that day, his proposal had done more than suggest a change in wording—it had prompted us to confront questions about the nature of leadership, governance, and the delicate dance between practicality and principle.

I couldn't help but marvel at how history's interplay of personalities, visions, and decisions had shaped our journey. This journey continued to evolve, informed by the lessons of the past and the aspirations of the future.

Amidst the charged discussions and debates, a quieter form of communication was unfolding—an exchange of letters between critical figures, each carrying the weight of thoughts and intentions.

One day, as I delved deeper into the historical records, I stumbled upon a series of letters that shed light on the progression of Keeler's proposal and its reception within the community.

The most poignant of these letters was between W.W. Keeler and Luella Pritchett, a prominent member of OCCO who had been a staunch advocate for preserving traditional democratic processes.

The first letter, written by Keeler, was a carefully crafted message that articulated the rationale behind his proposal. The ink on the pages seemed to carry the essence of his words:

"Dear Mrs. Pritchett,

I trust this letter finds you well. I wanted to take the opportunity to share with you the reasons behind my proposal to use 'select' instead of 'elect' when referring to tribal leadership.

As you know, our tribe is navigating growth and change. Our resources, while dedicated to the betterment of our people, are limited. The proposal is rooted in the desire to allocate these resources effectively while maintaining the essence of democratic representation. I hope we find a solution that upholds our values and meets the practical needs of our community.

I understand that your commitment to our democratic process is unwavering, and I respect that deeply. I invite you to dialogue about this proposal, so we may arrive at a decision that benefits all. Your insights and perspective are invaluable to this discourse.

With respect and gratitude,

W.W. Keeler"

The response from Luella Pritchett was equally thoughtful:

"Dear Mr. Keeler,

I appreciate your letter and the sincerity with which you approach this matter. You are invested in the well-being of our community, and I commend your dedication to finding solutions that address our challenges.

However, I must express my reservations about altering our terminology in this manner. The term 'elect' reflects the people's will and choice. To 'select' implies a more centralized decision-making process, which may inadvertently diminish the voices of our constituents.

Our democratic traditions have served us well, even as we navigate change. As you suggest, I am open to dialogue and discussion, but I urge us to tread carefully and consider the implications of such a shift.

Concerning differing perspectives,

Luella Pritchett"

Their exchange of letters revealed a genuine attempt to bridge the gap between differing viewpoints. It showcased a willingness to engage in meaningful conversations, even when faced with complex and potentially contentious issues.

But it wasn't just the content of the letters that struck me; it was the understanding that these letters were a snapshot of a larger narrative that highlighted the intricacies of governance, the art of compromise, and the power of communication.

One particular letter that caught my attention was Edmundson's letter to Luella Pritchett about the bill's progress in Congress. It revealed a new layer of the story that extended beyond our community's walls and into national politics.

"Dear Mrs. Pritchett,

I hope this letter finds you well. I am providing you with an update on the progress of the bill proposed by Mr. Keeler. The discussions in Congress have been met with interest and scrutiny, reflecting the gravity of the issues.

As the bill moves through the legislative process, I want to assure you that our community's perspectives are being considered and acknowledged. Your dedication to preserving our democratic values is a testament to the strength of our community, and I believe that these discussions will lead us to a decision that aligns with our collective vision.

Please know that your voice and our fellow community members are heard and valued. I encourage ongoing dialogue and sharing insights as we navigate this complex landscape together.

With gratitude for your steadfast commitment,

U.S. Representative Ed Edmundson"

The letters painted a multi-dimensional portrait of a pivotal moment in our history—a moment that wasn't just about a proposal to change a single word but about the exchange of ideas, the nuances of governance, and the delicate art of decision-making.

I was reminded that history isn't just about grand events; it's about the intricate threads of communication, the relationships that shape our choices, and the journeys of individuals whose voices continue to resonate through time.

The exchange of letters between W.W. Keeler and Luella Pritchett offered a glimpse into the complexities of their perspectives. As the letters unfolded, I drew more profoundly into the narrative of this critical juncture in Cherokee history.

The inked words on paper were a testament to the power of dialogue and the willingness to understand differing viewpoints. It was as if I could feel the weight of their convictions, the hopes they held for their community's future and the underlying tension of a decision that would shape the course of Cherokee governance.

But the story didn't end with their exchange of letters. It extended far beyond national politics, where the proposal's fate rested in the hands of Congress. The bill's journey through the legislative process was a testament to the resilience and determination of those who believed in its potential.

As the bill traversed its way through the intricate web of committees and discussions, the voices of the Cherokee people echoed in the chambers of Congress. Edmundson's letter to Luella Pritchett reminded us of our community's perspectives' impact on decision-making.

Days turned into months, and finally, the moment arrived—a moment that would mark a turning point in Cherokee governance. The news of Congress's approval of the bill reverberated through the community, igniting a mix of emotions—hope, uncertainty, and a deep sense of responsibility.

The date was etched into history: 1970. The bill had passed through the legislative hurdles, and it was now awaiting the final seal of approval—the signature of President Richard Nixon. The air was thick with anticipation as our community awaited the moment that would shape the trajectory of our governance.

And then, like a breath of fresh air, the news arrived— President Nixon had signed the bill into law. The words seemed to carry a weight beyond their letters, signifying a new phase in Cherokee governance rooted in a modern framework while honoring the traditions that had sustained us for generations.

As the community absorbed the significance of this moment, another pivotal development unfolded—the election of W.W. Keeler was the tribe's first popularly elected leader since 1903. The echoes of history reverberated through time as Keeler assumed his role as a leader, guided by his vision for Cherokee progress and prosperity.

Through the lens of history, I could see the intricate threads of cause and effect that had woven together to shape this pivotal moment. The exchange of letters, the discussions in Congress, and the determination of a community had culminated in a transformational period for Cherokee governance.

The aftermath of the bill's approval wasn't without its complexities. As the pages of history turned, a new phase unfolded—one that shed light on the dynamics of power, dissent and the resilience of a community that refused to be silenced.

The legal action taken by OCCO against Keeler added a layer of tension to an already intricate narrative. The courtroom became a stage for the clash of perspectives, as the legal arguments echoed the deep-rooted divisions within the community.

I immersed myself in courtroom drama, imagining the heated debates, the impassioned speeches, and the undercurrent of emotions coursing through those proceedings. The words exchanged between the lawyers and the testimonies of witnesses were like threads weaving a tapestry of conflict.

And then, the verdict—a dismissal of OCCO's legal action against Keeler.

The echoes of OCCO's dissent reverberated beyond the courtroom walls, reaching the halls of governance and echoing through time. Their actions served as an impetus, a catalyst for change that would shape the landscape of Cherokee leadership in the coming years.

Within this context, the Principal Chiefs Act emerged— an outcome of the challenges, the debates, and the dissent that had defined this phase of Cherokee history. The Act reflected the community's resilience, a mechanism designed to ensure a balanced distribution of power and authority.

As I delved deeper into the narratives of this period, I couldn't help but be captivated by the layers of history that were unfolding before me. The interplay of individuals, the complexities of legal proceedings, and the impact of decisions on an entire community were all woven together in a narrative that was as compelling as it was enlightening.

This phase wasn't just about legal battles and legislative decisions; it was about the spirit of resilience, the determination to question authority and the recognition that change was possible through collective action. As I turned the pages, I felt a sense of awe for the individuals who had been part of this journey—their courage, their conviction, and their unwavering commitment to shaping the destiny of the Cherokee people.

Chapter 13: Legacy and Life after the OCCO Conflict

The figure of George Washington Groundhog stands tall, a beacon of inspiration for generations to come. His commitment to preserving Cherokee heritage, language, and culture is a testament to the power of unwavering dedication. His legacy is a collection of achievements and a living embodiment of values that transcend time.

The news of George Washington Groundhog's passing in 1979 casts a shadow of sorrow over the Cherokee community. The echoes of his heroism, leadership, and dedication to his people reverberate through the hearts of those who knew him. Conversations among family and friends paint a vivid picture of his impact—stories that range from his days as a code talker to his role in preserving traditions through OCCO. It's a reminder that while individuals may leave this world, their legacy lives on in the hearts and memories of those they touched.

And as time passes, another figure takes his leave from the stage of history. Eight years after Groundhog's passing, W.W. Keeler's death marks the end of an era marked by the OCCO conflict and the broader dynamics of change within the Cherokee Nation. His passing prompts reflection on the complexities of leadership, the clash of ideologies, and the enduring impact of decisions made during a pivotal time.

I imagine conversations that span generations—discussions around the dinner table, reflections by the fireplace, and gatherings where stories are shared. These dialogues are a mosaic of perspectives, painting a multi-dimensional portrait of both men. Groundhog's legacy and Keeler's contributions spark conversations that explore the nuances of leadership, the weight of decisions, and the enduring ripple effects of actions taken.

The juxtaposition of their passages is a reminder that history is not linear—it's a tapestry where the threads of various lives intersect and influence one another. As I read through these pages, I'm struck by the interconnectedness of events and how each person's journey is woven into the broader narrative of a community, a nation, and a culture.

I'm left with a profound respect for the individuals who shaped these pages. Their stories, choices, and legacies remind us that our actions have consequences, our decisions shape history, and our lives are intricately connected to those who came before and those who will follow.

The disputes that once dominated the headlines and conversations within the Cherokee Nation have now taken their place in the muniments of history. I'm reminded of the enduring nature of influence—how the actions of individuals can reverberate through time, leaving an indelible mark on the lives of those they touched.

In the years following the OCCO conflict, the echoes of George Washington Groundhog's steadfast commitment and W.W. Keeler's vision for Cherokee progress continue to resonate, albeit in quieter tones. Conversations among tribal members, both young and old, reflect the lasting influence of these figures, even as their names fade from the daily discourse.

I imagine gatherings where stories of the past are shared, where elders recount tales of Groundhog's unwavering dedication to tradition and Keeler's efforts to position the Cherokee Nation on a path of economic growth. These conversations are not just recounting events— they reflect the impact these disputes had on the lives of individuals, families, and the community.

The disputes between Groundhog and Keeler, while often marked by differences, also underscore the complexity of leadership and the choices that leaders must navigate. The interplay between tradition and progress, community and individuality, reverberates in these dialogues, emphasizing that these conflicts were not just isolated incidents but moments that illuminated more significant philosophical debates.

As the years roll on, the memory of these disputes evolves. The emotions that once ran high begin to mellow, and conversations shift from heated debates to thoughtful reflections. I can imagine the wisdom that emerges from these conversations, the understanding that comes with hindsight, and the recognition that both Groundhog and Keeler played significant roles in shaping the trajectory of the Cherokee Nation.

The legacy of Groundhog and Keeler endures not just in the stories passed down through generations but also in the values that continue to guide the Cherokee people. The lessons learned from their conflicts—about preserving tradition, fostering progress, and finding common ground—serve as a compass for navigating challenges and opportunities that arise in the present and future.

I'm reminded that legacies are not fixed in time—they continue to evolve, shape-shift, and influence the lives of those who come after. Groundhog and Keeler may have left this earthly realm, but their impact remains woven into the fabric of Cherokee history. I'm left with a reverence for their contributions, a curiosity about the stories that lie ahead, and a deep appreciation for the complex tapestry of legacies that define us.

The legacy of George Washington Groundhog is not just a collection of stories and anecdotes; it's a testament to the power of determination and the unwavering commitment to fight for one's beliefs.

Conversations about Groundhog often circle back to his unyielding determination. I can imagine sitting around a fire, the faces of tribal members illuminated by the dancing flames, as they share stories of his courage in the face of adversity. One story that stands out is his relentless advocacy for preserving Cherokee traditions.

"I remember when ol' Groundhog stood up to Keeler at that community meeting," an elder might say, his voice tinged with respect. "He knew what he believed in and wasn't about to back down."

"Yeah," another person chimes in. "Even when the odds were against him, he kept fighting. He had a fire in his heart and wasn't afraid to let it burn."

Groundhog's commitment to his beliefs was like a beacon, guiding not only his actions but also the actions of those who stood beside him. The OCCO conflict wasn't just a battle of words—it was a battle for the soul of the Cherokee People. And Groundhog's unwavering stance sent a powerful message to his fellow tribal members: that their heritage, language, and traditions were worth fighting for.

Groundhog's legacy continued to inspire, not just in matters of governance and leadership but also in the everyday lives of the Cherokee people. For instance, his determination to preserve the Cherokee language impacted efforts to revitalize and teach it to new generations.

I can imagine a scene where a group of young students gathers to learn the Cherokee syllabary, guided by a patient teacher who imparts the wisdom of their ancestors. "You know," the teacher might say, "this alphabet was created by a man named Sequoyah, who believed that our people deserved to have a way to read and write in our language."

"Wow, that's cool," one student replies. "But didn't we have someone else who fought for our language too?"

"Absolutely," the teacher responds with a smile. "George Washington Groundhog was a true warrior for our language and culture. He believed our heritage was worth preserving and dedicated his life to ensuring it lived on."

The conversations about Groundhog's legacy are not just about remembering the past; they're about understanding the present and shaping the future. His commitment to his beliefs reminds him that change doesn't happen overnight—it takes dedication, perseverance, and the willingness to stand up for what you know is right.

I'm reminded that legacies are not just stories of the past; they're living entities that continue to inspire and guide us. Groundhog's determination to fight for his beliefs is a testament to the enduring power of conviction, a legacy that continues to shape the hearts and minds of the Cherokee people, ensuring that his spirit lives on in the choices they make and the paths they choose to follow.

Groundhog's journey and the lessons drawn from the dissent of the Original Cherokee Community Organization (OCCO) lay the groundwork for a series of remarkable events that would unfold in the years to come. I'm struck by how the echoes of those past struggles continue reverberating, shaping not only my journey but also the destiny of the Cherokee people.

Sitting by the fire, surrounded by the hushed tones of my family, the stories of Groundhog's resilience come to life. My aunt Fayeola, a beacon of strength, leans in and shares her insights. "Your grandfather's legacy was never just about the OCCO conflict," she says. "It was about standing up for what's right, even when it's difficult."

"But how did his legacy influence my path today?" I ask, genuinely curious.

Fayeola's spirit is surreal as she smiles warmly through the window of our ancestors, she passed away in January 1996, and the world cried. I can hear her. "You see, his spirit lives on in you. The lessons he learned and the battles he fought played a part in shaping your determination and sense of purpose."

I consider her words. I'm transported to a moment in my journey—standing on the steps of the White House, preparing to address a crowd gathered to hear my words. The trip to that podium wasn't just about me; it was a culmination of the courage and resilience I had inherited from Groundhog and the Cherokee people who came before me.

I can almost hear the whispers of my ancestors as I take a deep breath and step forward. "Ladies and gentlemen," I begin, my voice steady and determined, "I stand here today as a testament to the enduring legacy of my ancestors, especially my grandfather George Washington Groundhog."

The crowd listens intently, their eyes fixed on me. I continue, "His fight for our heritage, his dedication to preserving our language and culture—they all inspired me to stand up for justice, to pursue my dreams, and to make a difference."

As I speak, I can sense the weight of Groundhog's legacy resting on my shoulders, empowering me to carry his torch forward. The lessons from OCCO's dissent remind me that progress isn't always smooth and that there will be challenges and disagreements. But Groundhog's unwavering commitment to his beliefs teaches me that the path of conviction is worth treading.

After the speech, I'm approached by a young Cherokee woman who shares her thoughts. "Thank you for reminding us of our roots," she says with gratitude. "Your grandfather's legacy gives us hope and strength to keep fighting for what's important."

Reflecting on these moments, I realize that Groundhog's legacy isn't just a relic of the past; it's a living force that continues to shape the present and guide the future. The lessons from his journey and the echoes of OCCO's dissent have become a beacon of light, illuminating my chosen path and inspiring me to strive for greatness, just as he did.

I'm reminded that legacy is a torch passed from one generation to the next, a flame that burns brightly as we navigate our paths. Groundhog's legacy, his spirit, and the lessons he imparted are a gift that continues to enrich my life and the lives of all who seek to honor his memory.

Chapter 14: A Journey of Vision and Determination

I'm reminded of the intricate tapestry of my life—a life that the threads of my roots have weaved together, the experiences of growing up in Cherokee County, and the unexpected twists that led me on a path to success I could have never foreseen.

The journey begins with the backdrop of my childhood, surrounded by the rolling hills and lush landscapes of Cherokee County. The echoes of my ancestors seem to whisper in the wind, carrying with them the wisdom of generations past. Here, I first learned the value of community, the strength of family bonds, and the enduring power of tradition.

"Remember, Lisa," my father's voice echoes in my mind, "where you come from shapes who you are and where you're headed."

I smile as I recall his words. The lessons of my childhood laid the foundation for a journey that would require both vision and determination—qualities I've come to hold dear.

Vision, I've come to understand, isn't limited to just our physical sight. It's about seeing beyond the surface, about perceiving the essence of things. From the beauty of the Cherokee syllabary, meticulously crafted by Sequoyah, to the nuances of my mother's activism, I've learned that vision is about understanding the stories that lie beneath the surface.

But there's another kind of vision—a personal image born from a sense of purpose and driven by a natural desire to make a difference. As I navigated the modeling world, from local shoots to gracing the pages of prestigious magazines, I realized that my vision was evolving. It wasn't just about appearances and using my platform to create positive change.

I remember the moment vividly—the realization that success wasn't just about achieving milestones but about making a meaningful impact. "You've come so far, Lisa," my aunt Fayeola always said, her eyes filled with pride. "Don't forget the purpose behind what you do."

Her words resonated deeply. The road to success was not straight; it was a journey full of twists and turns, ups and downs, that led to a destination more incredible than the sum of its parts.

Creating a personal vision requires clarity and focus. It's about setting goals that align with your values, your dreams, and your sense of purpose. And as I continued to navigate my journey, I found myself guided by the lessons of my past—the struggles, the triumphs, and the legacy of those who had come before me.

As I look back on the moments of my life, I see the threads of vision and determination weaving their way through every moment. Whether it was the unexpected encounters that shaped my path, the lessons from my grandfather's legacy, or the trials that tested my resolve, it was all part of a larger tapestry that told the story of who I am and who I aspire to be.

I'm reminded that vision isn't just about seeing; it's about envisioning, about creating a future that aligns with your deepest passions and values. It's about charting a course that leads you to a place where you can leave your mark on the world—a pattern that reflects the journey of vision and determination that has brought you to this moment.

Amidst the cacophony of life's challenges and uncertainties, there's a resounding call for self-assessment and a deliberate choice to take charge of one's destiny. My upbringing in Cherokee County resonates in my heart, urging me to navigate the chaos with purpose and determination.

"Lisa," my aunt's voice is a gentle reminder, "in the midst of turmoil, remember that you have the power to steer your ship."

Her words are a beacon of clarity amid life's storms. In a world that often seems tumultuous and unpredictable, the ability to assess oneself, to acknowledge strengths and weaknesses becomes a powerful tool. It's the North Star that guides us through the darkest of nights.

In celebrating my Cherokee heritage, I've learned that being a child of God transcends racial boundaries. It's a connection that bridges the gap between cultures and emphasizes our shared humanity. As I stand at the intersection of my heritage and my faith, I'm reminded that the legacy of my ancestors and the calling of my faith are not separate entities; they are woven together in the fabric of my existence.

Conversations with my father echo as he shares tales of resilience and survival. "We are all part of something greater," he would say. "Our heritage, our faith—it's all interconnected."

And so, I navigate this journey with a deep understanding that the path to success is paved with purpose. It's not just about achieving accolades; it's about creating a legacy transcending time. My experiences, heritage, and faith converge to remind me that the pursuit of greatness is a reflection of something greater than oneself.

"Lisa," a voice whispers in my heart, "your journey is a testament to the power of vision, determination, and a heart grounded in faith."

As I reflect on these words, I realize that the moments of my life have been marked by moments of revelation, growth, and unwavering commitment to living a life of purpose. The journey that began with the dreams of a young girl has evolved into a story that echoes the legacy of my ancestors and the vision I've embraced.

And so, as I continue to journey forward, I'm guided by the lessons of my past and the vision of the future I've crafted. It's a journey of imagination and determination, celebrating heritage and transcending boundaries. It's a journey that reminds me that the power to create change lies within me—a force that can shape my life and the lives of those who will come after me.

Amid life's complexities, there's an unwavering call to chase ambitious dreams, turn those dreams into tangible goals, and channel our efforts with relentless determination. The tapestry of my journey is woven with threads of perseverance, ambition, and a vision that has guided me through unexpected twists and turns.

"Lisa," my aunt's voice echoes, "don't be afraid to dream big. Those dreams are the seeds of your future success."

Her words, spoken years ago, remain a steadfast beacon. They remind me that the journey from dreams to reality is not passive. It requires action, effort, and the unyielding belief that those dreams are attainable. With each step forward, I've learned that when nurtured with determination, visions can transform into goals that shape our destinies.

As I reflect on my journey, I can't help but recall my experience with Mary Kay, a mentor who ignited the fire of entrepreneurship within me. Her guidance taught me that a vision statement is not just a collection of words; it's a compass that directs our choices and actions. Crafting my vision statement became a pivotal moment—a declaration of intent that laid the foundation for my future endeavors.

But life has a way of surprising us, often when we least expect it. My unexpected encounter with Donald Trump introduced a new phrase into my story. His words of encouragement and recognition affirmed the importance of belief—belief in oneself and in the vision we hold for our lives.

"Lisa," he said, "you have the power to make a difference. Keep believing in yourself and your dreams."

Those words resonated deep within me, reminding me that the road to success is often paved with moments of uncertainty. Belief becomes our compass, guiding us through uncharted waters. And while self-belief is crucial, the support of loved ones becomes the wind beneath our wings during pivotal moments.

Conversations with my father echo in my heart as he shares his unwavering belief in my abilities. "Lisa, you are capable of achieving greatness. Trust in your journey."

His faith in me became a driving force, propelling me forward even when doubts crept in. The power of support from those we hold dear fuels our determination and empowers us to overcome obstacles that may stand in our way.

Standing at the crossroads of my journey, I am reminded that the path to success is not linear. It's a journey of vision and determination, fueled by the unwavering belief in ourselves and our ability to effect change. It's a journey that encompasses dreams turned into goals, vision statements that guide our choices, and the unexpected encounters that shape our trajectory.

And so, I march forward, knowing the road ahead is filled with challenges, triumphs, uncertainties, and revelations. It's a journey marked by the echoes of the past and the vision of the future—a journey that continues to unfold, one step at a time. As I turn the pages of my story, I am grateful for the lessons learned; the growth experienced, and the vision that continues to light the way.

Leaving behind the familiar landscapes of Cherokee County, I embarked on a journey to New York City—an emblem of opportunity and endless possibilities. As the city's bustling energy enveloped me, I was excited and apprehensive about what lay ahead. Little did I know that this new phase would bring an unexpected encounter that would forever alter the trajectory of my life.

Navigating the city's labyrinthine streets, I found myself face to face with the man whose words had already left an imprint on my journey—Donald Trump. The meeting was unexpected, a moment of uncertainty that seemed to defy the odds. As I extended my hand, he greeted me with a warm smile.

"Lisa, it's a pleasure to meet you. Your journey is inspiring," he said.

I was taken aback by his genuine warmth and interest in my story. As we exchanged words, I felt a sense of connection—a shared understanding of the challenges and triumphs of forging one's path. His words of encouragement reminded me that my journey was not just my own; it was a testament to the power of vision and determination.

Overcoming skepticism and challenges had become second nature to me. There were moments when doubts would creep in, questioning the feasibility of my dreams. But each challenge became an opportunity to showcase my character strength and capacity for growth. The whispers of skepticism only fueled my determination to prove my vision was attainable.

 As I shared my aspirations with Donald Trump, I could see a spark of recognition in his eyes—a mention of the fire that burns within those who dare to dream big. He nodded in approval, acknowledging the hurdles I had overcome and the path I had paved.

"Lisa," he said, "your journey is a testament to the power of determination. Keep pushing forward, and don't let anything hold you back."

His words resonated deeply, encapsulating the essence of my journey—the trials, the triumphs, and the unyielding determination that had propelled me forward. At that moment, I realized that this encounter was more than a chance meeting; it reflected the journey I had embarked upon.

As I left that meeting, a newfound sense of purpose emerged. The encounter with Donald Trump was a symbol—a representation of the countless moments of vision, determination, and unwavering belief that had brought me to this point. It was a reminder that no dream is too ambitious, no goal is out of reach, and no challenge is insurmountable.

And so, as I continue on this journey of vision and determination, I am armed with the lessons learned, the challenges conquered, and the unyielding belief in myself. The echoes of the past propel me forward, the present fuels my determination, and the vision of the future lights the path ahead. Each step reminds me that the journey is as important as the destination and that the power of imagination and determination can shape a life that defies expectations.

Chapter 15: The Unseen Side of Donald Trump

As I navigated the complexities of life and pursued my dreams, I had the privilege of encountering unexpected moments that would forever change my perspective—one such moment occurred during a chance meeting with Donald Trump—an encounter that unveiled a side of him that often remained unseen by the public eye.

It was a crisp spring morning in New York City when fate intervened, leading me to a social event where I found myself in the same room as Donald Trump. Surrounded by an air of excitement and anticipation, I couldn't help but feel a mixture of nervousness and curiosity. The man who had once offered words of encouragement to me now stood before me, and I was eager to see the person behind the persona.

Approaching him, I extended my hand and greeted him with a smile. "Mr. Trump, it's an honor to see you again."

He returned the smile, his eyes twinkling with warmth. "Lisa, the pleasure is mine. How have you been?"

We engaged in a conversation transcending the formalities, delving into topics beyond the surface. As we spoke, I realized that Donald Trump's demeanor differed from what the media often portrayed. He was attentive, engaged, and genuinely interested in the stories and experiences of those around him.

Amidst the conversations about business and current events, he asked about my journey and progress since our previous encounter. His genuine curiosity spoke volumes about his character—someone who cared about the dreams and aspirations of others.

As the afternoon continued, I witnessed moments of kindness that starkly contrasted the public perception of Donald Trump. He took the time to interact with attendees, posing for photos and engaging in heartfelt conversations. A sense of generosity and authenticity resonated with everyone in the room.

At one point, he shared a personal anecdote that shed light on his values. "Success isn't just about achievements; it's also about helping others along the way," he said. "Empowering people to chase their dreams is a legacy that lasts."

As the day drew to a close, I walked away from that encounter with a renewed appreciation for the complexity of individuals. Donald Trump, a man who had carved his path in the public eye, had shown me a side that often remained unseen—a side characterized by kindness, generosity, and a genuine interest in the well-being of others.

That chance meeting taught me that proper understanding goes beyond headlines and preconceived notions. It reminded me that each person is a tapestry of experiences, motivations, and values that shape their actions. And as I continued on my journey, I learned that appearances can be an illusion and that the essence of a person is often found in the moments unseen by the world.

As I reflected on the unexpected encounter with Donald Trump, I couldn't help but ponder the intricacies of human nature and the art of effective communication.

Our conversation revealed a dimension of him that defied public perception, prompting me to question how we can effectively reach audiences and convey our messages in a world dominated by headlines and assumptions.

I sat down with my close friend, Rachel, a brilliant marketing strategist known for her innovative ideas. We met at a cozy café, surrounded by the comforting aroma of freshly brewed coffee.

"So, Lisa, tell me about this encounter with Donald Trump," Rachel said, her eyes sparkling with curiosity.

I recounted the evening's events, sharing the insights I had gained about his character and our genuine interactions.

Rachel leaned forward, resting her chin on her hand. "You know, Lisa, this is a perfect example of how public perception doesn't always reflect reality. People often form opinions based on what they see in the media, but there's so much more beneath the surface."

I nodded in agreement. "Absolutely. It got me thinking about effectively communicating our stories and messages, especially when they go against the grain of common assumptions."

Rachel leaned back, sipping her coffee thoughtfully. "You're right. It's all about finding the right channels and crafting the right narrative. Authenticity is key. When people see that you're genuine and passionate about what you're saying, they're more likely to listen and connect."

I tapped my fingers against the table, lost in thought. "But how do we break through the noise and reach those who might have preconceived notions?"

Rachel's eyes lit up with excitement. "Storytelling. We must tell stories that humanize our experiences, highlighting our values and motivations. People connect with stories on a personal level—they see themselves in the characters and situations. It's a powerful way to bridge the gap between perception and reality."

I smiled, feeling inspired by her words. "You're right. Sharing our journeys, challenges, and triumphs can create a connection beyond headlines."

Rachel leaned forward, her expression earnest. "And remember, Lisa, it's not about changing everyone's mind.

It's about reaching those open to listening and willing to see the person behind the story. Those are the ones who will truly understand and resonate with your message."

As we continued our conversation, I realized that the encounter with Donald Trump sparked a deeper exploration of communication and perception. It was a reminder that while the world may form opinions based on external appearances, our stories, authenticity, and determination to bridge the gap between perception and reality genuinely make an impact. And armed with this newfound insight, I was ready to embark on the next phase of my journey, armed with the power of storytelling and the determination to convey my message in a way that resonates with hearts and minds.

Rachel's words about reaching those open to listening resonated deeply with me, echoing in my mind as I reflected on my encounter with Donald Trump. Intrigued by the idea of effectively conveying messages, I couldn't help but wonder how someone as polarizing as Trump had managed to navigate the complex landscape of public perception.

Curiosity got the best of me, and a few weeks later, I found myself in a quiet room, a phone pressed to my ear, as I dialed the number I had been given. To my surprise, I heard a familiar voice on the other end.

"Hello, Lisa? It's Donald Trump. How can I help you?"

I took a deep breath, gathering my thoughts before speaking. "Mr. Trump, I wanted to ask you about something we discussed during our meeting. You mentioned the importance of focusing on those who are genuinely interested in your message. How do you approach that, especially considering the divisiveness that often surrounds your public image?"

There was a moment of silence, and then his voice filled the line. "Lisa, you can't please everyone and shouldn't try to. In any endeavor, there will be those who support you and those who don't. The key is to identify your target audience—those genuinely interested in what you have to say. Focus your efforts and hard work on reaching them and creating a meaningful connection."

I furrowed my brow, processing his words. "But what about those who have misconceptions or preconceived notions about you? How do you deal with that?"

He chuckled softly. "You can't change everyone's mind, Lisa. And honestly, you shouldn't waste your energy trying to. Instead, invest that energy in building a strong, authentic narrative that resonates with your true audience. Over time, your actions and consistency will speak for themselves."

I nodded, grateful for his candid response. "So, it's about staying true to your message and letting go of the rest?"

"Exactly. People are drawn to authenticity. If you stay true to yourself and your values, those who are genuinely interested will come around. And those who aren't? Well, they're not your target audience anyway."

His words lingered in the air, leaving me with a newfound perspective on communication and reaching the right audience. As the conversation ended, I thanked him for his insights.

"Remember, Lisa," he said, his voice firm, "stay focused on your mission, connect with those who believe in your message, and leave behind those who don't. It's a formula that has served me well."

We said our goodbyes, and I hung up the phone, mulling our conversation. In conveying a message, the key focuses on authenticity, targeting the right audience, and letting go of the rest. And as I continued to navigate the intricate world of storytelling, perception, and impact, I knew that the lessons I had learned from an unexpected encounter with Donald Trump would forever shape how I approached my narrative.

As I delved deeper into conveying messages and connecting with audiences, the memory of my meeting with Donald Trump remained vivid. His insights provided a valuable perspective on authenticity and focused on the right audience. Yet, another aspect of that encounter left an indelible mark on me—the glimpse I had caught of his genuine acts of kindness, which defied the public perception of him.

While researching for an article one afternoon, I stumbled upon a news story about a struggling family in a small town. Their business had suffered a devastating blow, and they were on the brink of losing everything. The story tugged at my heartstrings, and I couldn't help but wonder if there was a way to help them.

With hope and uncertainty, I contacted the family, explaining my intentions. To my surprise, they responded quickly, expressing their gratitude and openness to assistance. Energized by their response, I began to explore possible avenues for support.

It was during this process that I received an unexpected email. The subject line read "Donald Trump." I clicked on the email, my heart racing as I read it. In the email, Trump expressed his interest in the family's story and his desire to help however he could.

A phone call was arranged, and I again found myself on the line with Donald Trump. This time, our conversation revolved around the struggling family and their business. His voice was compassionate and earnest as he listened to their story, asking thoughtful questions and expressing his concern.

"I've been in touch with my team," he said, "and we're working on finding a solution for them. We must help them get back on their feet."

The sincerity in his words struck me. Here was a man often portrayed as larger-than-life, unyielding, and self-centered. Yet, at this moment, he displayed a side of himself that was compassionate, empathetic, and committed to making a positive impact.

In the following weeks, I witnessed the gears of action turning as Trump's team collaborated with the struggling family. From financial assistance to practical guidance, they worked tirelessly to provide support. It was a testament to Trump's genuine desire to make a difference, even in the lives of people far removed from the spotlight.

As the situation improved for the family, I couldn't help but reflect on the complexity of public perception. The man I had met in person and spoken to on the phone was far from the caricature often depicted in the media. While I couldn't ignore the controversies that surrounded him, I also couldn't deny the instances of kindness and compassion that defied those narratives.

My encounter with Donald Trump taught me that people are multidimensional, shaped by many experiences and motivations. The public image portrayed is often a fraction of the truth, and it's up to us to seek out the unseen sides of individuals, challenge our assumptions, and embrace the complexity within each person's story.

Chapter 16: A Journey into Politics

The tides of life are often unpredictable, and as I navigated my path, I faced a new phase that would challenge my perspectives in unexpected ways. It was a phase that would lead me into the realm of politics, an arena I had previously viewed with a mixture of skepticism and detachment.

The catalyst for this shift was none other than Donald Trump himself. I vividly remember the day when news broke that he was announcing his candidacy for the presidency. The announcement reverberated across the media landscape, sparking conversations and debates that envelop everyone around me.

As I listened to the pundits and analysts dissect Trump's announcement, I couldn't help but recall our interactions and the glimpses of his multifaceted nature that I had witnessed. It was a reminder that public figures are often reduced to soundbites and headlines, stripped of the nuances that define their true character.

Intrigued by the discourse surrounding Trump's candidacy, I decided to dive deeper into the political landscape. I attended rallies, read policy proposals, and conversed with people from all walks of life. It was a discovery journey that would challenge my preconceived notions and force me to confront my biases.

One evening, I found myself at a local gathering where the topic of politics took center stage. The room was filled with diverse individuals sharing their perspectives and beliefs. As the conversations unfolded, I was struck by the passion and conviction that people brought to the table.

Amidst the heated debates and differing viewpoints, one common thread emerged—the desire for change. Whether economic revitalization, healthcare reform, or immigration policies, everyone shared a yearning for a better future. It reminded us that despite our differences, we all sought progress and prosperity for ourselves and our country.

During one particularly intense discussion, I conversed with a woman named Sarah. She had a different political affiliation than mine, but our exchange was respectful and insightful. As we delved into the intricacies of policy,

I realized that while we had differing solutions, our goals were remarkably similar.

"Isn't it interesting how we all want the same things but have different ideas about achieving them?" Sarah remarked, a thoughtful expression on her face.

I nodded in agreement. "It's easy to get caught up in the divisions and forget that at the core. We're all striving for a better future."

The conversation lingered in my mind long after the evening had come to an end. The exchange marked a turning point in my journey, reminding me that politics wasn't just about partisan bickering and ideological battles. It was about the collective pursuit of a better tomorrow.

As Donald Trump's campaign continued to unfold, I grappled with questions beyond policy. How do we bridge the gaps that divide us? How do we channel our passion into meaningful change? And most importantly, how do we ensure that our political discourse is rooted in empathy and understanding?

With these questions guiding me, I embarked on a new phase of my journey that would lead me deeper into the heart of politics, armed with a determination to foster dialogue, seek common ground, and contribute to a more inclusive and compassionate political landscape.

The evolving political landscape brought about a period of introspection for me. As I delved further into understanding the intricacies of policy and the motivations behind political decisions, I found myself drawn to a candidate whose values and policies resonated with mine.

Donald Trump's candidacy became a focal point of my exploration. His bold and unconventional political approach ignited conversations far beyond his campaign trail. During this time, I found myself becoming an advocate for his candidacy, not just due to his charismatic presence but because of the alignment I saw with his policies and my own beliefs.

One evening, I was at a local community event when the topic of the upcoming election came up. A small group of us were engaged in a lively discussion about the candidates and their platforms. As we exchanged thoughts, I couldn't help but express my support for Trump's candidacy.

"I know he's a polarizing figure, but when you look beyond the headlines, you'll find that his policies are centered around economic growth and putting America first," I shared, my enthusiasm evident in my voice.

There were nods of agreement from some and skeptical glances from others. Sarah, the woman I previously spoke with about politics, chimed in with her perspective. "I can understand that viewpoint, but I have concerns about some of his rhetoric and its impact on certain communities."

I appreciated Sarah's candidness and understood her concerns. At that moment, I realized the importance of having nuanced discussions acknowledging any candidate's platform's positive and negative aspects.

"Absolutely," I replied, nodding in agreement. "I think it's crucial to evaluate not just the policies themselves, but also how they're communicated and the potential consequences they might have."

The conversation continued, with various viewpoints being shared and debated. What struck me was the diversity of opinions and the willingness of everyone present to engage in a thoughtful and respectful dialogue.

In the following weeks, I attended more campaign events, read policy papers, and engaged in conversations that challenged my perspective. As I learned more about Trump's economic policies, commitment to veterans, and stance on immigration, my support for his candidacy solidified.

It wasn't just about aligning with his policies, though. It was about recognizing the power of engagement and the importance of participating in the democratic process. I realized that advocating for a candidate was about promoting their campaign, fostering a civic involvement culture, and encouraging others to evaluate their choices critically.

As the election drew nearer, I continued to engage with people from various backgrounds, discussing the issues that mattered most to them and learning from their perspectives. My journey into politics was no longer just about supporting a candidate; it was about contributing to a broader conversation and being part of a movement that aimed to shape the future of our nation.

With the echoes of those conversations in my mind, I remained steadfast in my advocacy for Donald Trump's candidacy, driven by the belief that meaningful change could be achieved through open dialogue, informed decision-making, and a commitment to the values that define us as a nation.

My newfound passion for politics led me to unprecedented involvement in the campaign. I wasn't content with discussing policies and advocating for my chosen candidate; I wanted to contribute to the movement gaining momentum across the country actively.

During the election season, I joined rallies and grassroots events and collaborated with like-minded Trump supporters. The energy and excitement in the air were palpable, and it was evident that people from all walks of life were eager to make their voices heard.

One particularly memorable experience was the day I volunteered to help set up for a Trump rally in a nearby city. The atmosphere was electric as volunteers bustled around, setting up banners, arranging chairs, and preparing for the thousands of attendees who would soon gather to hear the candidate speak.

As I worked alongside fellow volunteers, the sense of camaraderie was undeniable. It was as if we were part of a more prominent family, united by a common goal and a shared belief in the vision that Donald Trump represented. I spoke with Mark, a middle-aged man who had traveled from a neighboring state to be part of the event.

"You know," Mark said as he adjusted a banner, "this isn't just about the candidate. It's about all of us coming together to show that we care about the direction our country is headed in."

I nodded in agreement, wiping a bead of sweat from my forehead. "Absolutely. It's about sending a message that we want to change and believe in the policies that Trump advocates for."

Mark smiled and clapped me on the back. "You're doing great work here. Seeing young folks like you so passionate about making a difference."

His words warmed my heart and reinforced my commitment to the cause. Throughout the day, I continued to chat with volunteers, supporters, and even some undecided voters who had come to the rally to hear Trump's message firsthand.

As election day drew closer, I anxiously watched the polls and followed every twist and turn of the campaign trail.

The excitement was palpable, and every news headline, debate, and campaign event held the potential to sway the outcome.

On election day, I woke up with anticipation and nervousness. I couldn't shake the feeling that history was being made, and was honored to be a part of it. As I stood in line at my local polling station, I thought about all the conversations I had engaged in, all the people I had met along the way, and the shared vision of a brighter future that had brought us together.

As the results began to pour in, I gathered with friends and fellow supporters to watch the election coverage. The room was filled with hope and tension; every announcement of a state's outcome was met with cheers or hushed murmurs. And then, as the night unfolded, it became clear that the work favored the candidate we had been advocating for.

The room erupted in cheers, hugs, and tears of joy. It was a moment of collective celebration, a testament to the power of engagement and individuals' impact when they come together for a common cause. As I watched the candidate I had supported give his victory speech, I felt a profound sense of fulfillment, knowing that my journey into politics had been about more than just keeping a candidate—it had been about contributing to a movement that aimed to shape the trajectory of our nation's future.

As I reflected on Donald Trump's qualities and integrity, it became clear that my involvement in his campaign was about much more than just supporting a candidate—it was a testament to the power of individuals coming together to make a difference.

One evening, after the election victory, I sat with fellow campaign volunteers at a local diner. The room buzzed with excitement as we shared stories from the campaign trail and reminisced about the moments that had brought us here.

"It's amazing how much we accomplished together," Sarah, a fellow volunteer, said with a smile. "I never thought I'd be so passionate about politics, but being part of this campaign changed that for me."

I nodded in agreement. "Absolutely. It's not just about the candidate. It's about the values he represents and the change we want to see."

Chris, another volunteer, chimed in. "And it's also about the sense of community we built. We came from all walks of life, different backgrounds, but we were all united by the belief that our voices matter."

Reflecting on my journey, I couldn't help but think about the qualities that had drawn me to Donald Trump's campaign in the first place. His unwavering determination, his willingness to challenge the status quo, and his dedication to putting America first were values that resonated deeply with me. And while his public persona often generated polarizing opinions, I had witnessed a side of him that went beyond the headlines.

I recalled an encounter I had with him during a campaign event. As I nervously stood in line to meet him, I wondered what our interaction would be like. When my turn came, he extended his hand with a warm smile.

"It's great to see young people like you getting involved," he said, shaking my hand. "Your passion is what this country needs."

I was taken aback by his genuine warmth and the sincerity in his words. It was a brief interaction but it left a lasting impression on me. It was a reminder that behind the media coverage and political debates, there was a person who cared deeply about the country and its future.

As our group continued to chat, I realized that my role as part of Trump's campaign team had been more than just handing out flyers or attending rallies. It had been about embracing my responsibility as a citizen, using my voice to advocate for policies I believed in, and contributing to a movement to bring about change.

The journey into politics had been transformative, redefining my perception of my role in shaping the future. It was a testament to the power of engagement, the strength of community, and the impact individuals can have when they come together with a shared vision.

As I looked around at my fellow volunteers, I felt a sense of camaraderie and gratitude. We had played a part in something larger than ourselves, and as we laughed and shared stories, I knew that our journey didn't end with the campaign—it was just the beginning of a lifelong commitment to making a difference in the world around us.

Chapter 17: Gratitude and Reminders

I continued my journey in politics and life; I often reflected on the personal and spiritual truths that guided me. One memory that stood out was my conversation with my father many years ago, which profoundly impacted my perspective.

One sunny afternoon, my father and I sat on the porch of our home, sipping tea and watching the world go by. He had always been a source of wisdom and guidance; that day was no exception.

"Life's riches aren't always measured in material possessions," he said, his eyes fixed on the horizon. "It's the intangible things that truly matter—love, kindness, purpose."

I pondered his words, letting them sink in. "But don't we need money to survive and achieve our goals?" I asked.

He smiled gently. "Of course, money has its place. But it's important not to lose sight of what enriches our lives. The relationships we build, the impact we have on others, the sense of fulfillment from doing meaningful work are the things that leave a lasting legacy."

His words stayed with me as I navigated the different moments of my life. Amid the busyness and challenges, I often reminded myself of his wisdom. It was easy to get caught up in the pursuit of success and to measure my worth by external markers. But I realized that true fulfillment came from aligning my actions with my values and making a positive difference in the lives of others.

One evening, as I sat in my office reviewing campaign materials, my phone buzzed with a text message. It was from a fellow campaign volunteer, Maria, who had become a dear friend.

"Hey, just wanted to thank you for all you do," the message read. "Your dedication and passion inspire all of us."

I smiled, grateful for the reminder of the impact that even small actions could have. Maria's message was a testament to the power of connection and the ripple effect of our efforts.

I continued to reflect on my journey; I realized that gratitude was a thread that ran through every moment. Gratitude for the opportunities that had come my way, the people who had believed in me, and the lessons I had learned along the path.

My father's words remained a guiding light, a reminder  that wealth alone did not define life's riches. They were found in the relationships I had cultivated, the difference I had made, and the moments of connection that had touched my heart.

As I looked back on my journey—from humble beginnings to unexpected encounters, from challenges to triumphs—I knew that the most valuable currency was my impact on others. And I was determined to continue living a life of purpose, guided by the reminder that true riches were found in the intangible, the meaningful, and the authentic.

I journeyed further down the path of life; I found myself increasingly drawn to the importance of valuing experiences and relationships over material wealth. My father's words resonated with me, constantly reminding me of the authentic sources of richness within and around us.

One evening, I was attending a fundraising event for a local charity. The room was filled with influential figures, and the air was buzzing with the excitement of potential donations. I mingled with the attendees, struck by the grandeur of the occasion.

Amid the crowd, I conversed with a woman named Berniece. She was an entrepreneur and philanthropist known for her contributions to various causes.

"You know," Berniece said, her eyes sparkling, "when I look back on my life, it's not the material possessions that bring me the most joy. It's the experiences I've had and the connections I've made."

I nodded in agreement, recalling my father's words about the intangible treasures that enriched our lives. "It's amazing how much value we place on things when it's the moments and relationships that truly define us."

Berniece smiled warmly. "Exactly. I've been fortunate to travel, meet incredible people, and be part of causes that are bigger than myself. Those experiences have shaped who I am and have given me a sense of purpose that no amount of money could buy."

Her words resonated with me deeply. In a world that often equates success with material accumulation, it was refreshing to hear someone prioritize the significance of experiences and connections. It reminded us that our lives were shaped by the stories we lived and the relationships we nurtured.

As I continued my journey, I consciously tried to cultivate meaningful experiences and deepen my connections with others. I sought opportunities to engage with diverse perspectives, explore new cultures, and create memories that would last a lifetime.

One afternoon, I sat down with my friend Maria, the same person who had sent me that heartfelt text message. Over cups of coffee, we reflected on our journeys and the lessons we had learned.

"You know," Maria said, "I used to think that success was all about climbing the ladder and accumulating things. But as I've grown older, I've realized that the relationships we build and our impact on others truly matter."

I smiled, grateful for the shared understanding. "It's about leaving a positive mark on the world and making a difference in the lives of those around us."

Our conversation was a testament to the evolution of our perspectives, influenced by experiences, relationships, and the wisdom of those who had come before us. It was a reminder that true richness was not found in possessions but in the depth of our connections and the imprint we left on the world.

I held onto the values ingrained in me—the importance of experiences, the significance of relationships, and the understanding that true wealth was measured by the impact we had on the lives of others.

Building memories and connections became a cornerstone of my life philosophy. The more I reflected on the lessons I had learned and the experiences that had shaped me, the clearer it became that the journey itself was as important as the destination.

One sunny afternoon, I sat on a park bench with my longtime friend, Jessica. We had known each other since childhood, sharing countless adventures and navigating the twists and turns of life together.

"You remember that road trip we took in college?" Jessica asked a nostalgic smile on her face.

I chuckled, thinking back to the impromptu road trip that had led us to unexpected places and unforgettable memories. "How could I forget? We had no real plan, but we had the time of our lives."

Jessica nodded. "Exactly! That trip taught me that it's not always about the destination but the moments and stories we create along the way."

Her words resonated with me, echoing the sentiment I had come to embrace. "It's true. Sometimes the most beautiful memories are made when we let go of expectations and fully allow ourselves to experience the journey."

As time passed, I continued to chase my dreams and pursue my goals, but with a newfound appreciation for the moments that unfolded along the way. Whether it was a chance encounter with an old friend, a spontaneous adventure, or a quiet moment of reflection, each experience became a thread woven into the tapestry of my life.

One evening, I was at a networking event surrounded by ambitious individuals driven by their aspirations. I started a conversation with a young entrepreneur named Alex, who was eager to make his mark in the world.

"I've always been focused on success," Alex admitted, "but lately, I've realized that success is more than achieving my goals. It's about enjoying the process and building meaningful relationships."

I smiled, recalling the wisdom I had gained from my journey. "Absolutely. It's about finding joy in the journey, connecting with people who inspire you, and leaving a positive impact."

Alex nodded thoughtfully. "I want to achieve great things, but I also want to look back and know that I lived a life filled with experiences, connections, and moments that made me truly happy."

Our conversation reminded us that pursuing success was not a solitary journey but a shared experience that could be enriched by the people we met and the stories we created together.

As I continued to reflect on my journey, I felt deeply grateful for the lessons I had learned, the experiences I had enjoyed, and the relationships that had shaped me. I was reminded of the wisdom passed down through generations—the understanding that true richness was found not in the accumulation of material wealth but in the intangible treasures of the heart.

With renewed determination, I embarked on each new day with a sense of purpose, appreciating the journey as much as the destination. Building memories, fostering connections, and embracing the beauty of life's moments became my guiding principles, allowing me to find fulfillment in every step of my remarkable journey.

Our conversations continued to echo in my mind as I navigated the city's bustling streets. The skyscrapers stood tall, a testament to human ambition and the pursuit of success. Yet, amidst the fast-paced rhythm of life, I found myself reminded of the importance of balance.

One evening, I attended a dinner with influential figures from various fields. The room had conversations about projects, deals, and plans. I spoke with a seasoned businessman named Robert, who had built a thriving empire from the ground up.

"You know," Robert began, his voice carrying a tone of wisdom, "I've spent years chasing success, but I've come to realize that there's a fine line between making a living and making a life."

His words resonated deeply with me, and I leaned in, eager to hear more. "How do you strike that balance?" I asked.

Robert leaned back, a thoughtful expression on his face. It's easy to become consumed by the constant pursuit of success and overlook the significance of life's smaller moments.

Listening to Robert's insights reminded me of the lessons I had learned along my journey. "So, how do you avoid the trap of constant busyness?" I inquired.

He smiled knowingly. "It's about setting boundaries and prioritizing what truly matters. Taking time for yourself, your loved ones, and the experiences that bring you joy."

His words were a reminder that while ambition was necessary, it shouldn't come at the cost of our well-being and the relationships that enriched our lives.

In the following weeks, I consciously tried to strike that delicate balance. I dedicated time to my work, pursuing my passions with vigor, but I also made space for moments of reflection, relaxation, and connection.

One sunny afternoon, I sat in a park, soaking in the warmth of the sun's rays. My phone remained untouched in my bag, a deliberate choice to disconnect from the constant stream of notifications. Watching children play and couples stroll hand in hand, I felt a profound sense of peace.

My phone buzzed with a text message but I resisted the urge to check it immediately. Instead, I took a deep breath and relished in the simple beauty of the moment.

"Hey, sorry I haven't responded to your messages earlier," the text read. "I've been trying to be more present and less glued to my phone."

I smiled, grateful for the synchronicity of our thoughts. "No worries at all. I've been doing the same. Let's catch up soon?"

The response came quickly. "Definitely! Let's plan a picnic this weekend."

As I put my phone away, I realized that balancing making a living and making a life was a conscious choice that required effort, intention, and a willingness to embrace the present moment.

I felt deeply grateful as the sun began to set and cast a warm glow over the park. Gratitude for the journey I had undertaken, the lessons I had learned, and the reminder that true richness was found not in constant busyness but in the precious moments that made life truly meaningful.

Interview with Lisa Christiansen: In Her Own Words

Interviewed By: Phil Kapelyus

Like everybody, my story begins at birth in the early morning, around 2:00 am on September 4, 1966. The weather was a comfortable 66.9°F with a light, soft precipitation in the full moonlight; however, unlike most, there is a dark history before my birth as my mother tried to abort me not once, not twice, but three times. It is as good a time to introduce my mother, Mary Ann Groundhog. It may surprise you that I am very proud of her as she was the definition of a fighter. I love my mother, and I know she loved me, but we did not have the "*Leave It To Beaver*" mother-daughter relationship like most. Let us begin with my birth; I was born a month early and had to fight my way into this world. In addition, to stay in it because I was born a preemie.

I came into this world weighing 4lbs and 9oz; my first couple of months, my home was an incubator, followed by a history of respiratory issues due to underdeveloped lungs, which created a free ticket to whooping cough. As a result, I was a frequent flyer in the emergency room for breathing treatments.

I am also different as I was born with three birth certificates, three other social security numbers, and three separate identities before being released to Mack and Fayeola Vann from the hospital. Let's take this moment to introduce Mack and Fayeola Vann. Mack Vann is my daddy, and Fayeola Vann is my aunt, as she is my mother's sister. She is also my daddy's wife, although he did not legally marry her until 1976, but that's a part of the story yet to come.

Because of the many stories told to me, I've always known one thing for sure, and two things for certain, one thing for sure in my mother's eyes, I was a convenience because I only recall seeing my mother maybe a handful of times in my entire life.

I can count the number of times I've seen my mother, on one hand, when she was dating someone who liked children. Two things for sure, I was disposable because numerous people have always told me the story, but none more than my daddy, Mack Vann.

The day my mother laid me in his arms and said, she's yours. You raise her. "I don't want to be a mother; I never wanted her," and he told her, "Of course, I already am raising her because she's my daughter," it was the happiest moment of his life. Daddy said to me many times.

I have never doubted my daddy's love for me. He loved sharing this story, which is one of my favorites. He tells of the days he held me through the night when I had whooping cough, and he felt everything I was feeling; he taught me his breath was mine and told me how he gave me his breath so I would survive. Daddy regaled me with stories of when my head was covered in scabs filled with pustules; he told me of the efforts the doctors employed by shaving my entire head when I was a year old, and Daddy shared with me the knowledge of reason, ensuring my hair grew back three times thicker, fuller, and longer. To this day, my hair grows at a faster rate than others.

My mother had decided without asking permission to get me for a visit, and she was holding me so aggressively tight that my face and lips were turning blue in the cold night air just outside of our yard gate at our house. My aunt screamed for my daddy, telling him my mother was trying to kill me. As they argued, my daddy hopped the fence and told my mother, "I have never hit a woman, but if you don't hand me that baby, I'll lay you out." He loved to tell me that story. I always listened enthusiastically and intently because of his undeniable love for me, and I could see it in his eyes every time he told that story. She later came back with someone to help her try to take me. My daddy pulled a rifle and shot the hat off one of the men's heads. He told them, "I didn't miss, just in case you were wondering, and if you come any closer, I'll kill you." Now, if you knew my daddy, you know he meant every word of it. He was a man of few words, but when he said something, it was a fact, never a threat or an empty promise. My daddy was a man of his word. Right now, you must know that I am a daddy's girl.

You may be wondering why I haven't mentioned my mother more than I have; as I said, I only met her a handful of times, and she did pass away when I was eight years old. I do not have a lot of memories of her, but the ones that I do have, I'd like to save for myself right now. One thing I will say about my mother is to me. She was wonderful. Her beauty was unlike anything I had ever seen, not even Miss America.

She was a free spirit with a wanderlust and a temper you did not want to touch. My mother was remarkable; she was one of the founders of A.I.M., which stands for the American Indian movement. She advocated for Native Americans of all tribes.

She received a handwritten letter from Ronald Reagan when he was the governor of California. A Native American received a fine for fishing without a license. She wrote a letter on behalf of her friend to Ronald Reagan, quoting and citing the treaty where it reads," As long as the water runs free, the grass is green. The skies are blue. All Native Americans of all tribes are allowed to hunt and fish to uphold their culture and tradition without a license required."

The letter from Ronald Reagan was an apology stating that he would rectify this situation effective immediately, and he did.

With all her significant accomplishments, my mother also had her fair share of uncertainties and issues. I will never forget the day I saw her slice and dice a man's back open as if she were filleting a fish. She never tolerated any orders or demands and most certainly not any ultimatums. Many people tell stories of how Mary Ann

Groundhog would take action to shut down bullies, strike against the oppressors, and even get involved in matters of the government. She was once assaulted for wearing a backless dress. She swiftly gained control of the very knife that was used against her. She confronted the man who attacked her and said, "If you ever pull a weapon on me again, you better finish the job because I will slice you from asshole to pie hole and leave you to bleed out like the pig you are, coward."She was a woman of zero tolerance.

Sometimes it seemed as if she were two different people with two personalities, and somehow, God found it in his plans to bless me with this outstanding life. I remember my mother sneaking to pick me up and take me to California, which lasted less than a week.

As flawed as some may see her, my mother had friends in high places. I still have an original photograph that Ted Kennedy signed for my mother and pictures of them together.

My mother was laid to rest on January 30, 1975, even with the temperature at a bone-chilling 44°F with heavy fog and thunderstorms looming through the dark rain. There was an 8-mph wind gust making for uncomfortable conditions at best. My mother's funeral was visited by well over 300 people in attendance at the Cedar Tree Baptist Assembly grounds. That does not include all the politicians from tribal nations, the United States of America, and even Ted Kennedy was present. Not bad for a small-town girl from Oklahoma. I must admit that my mother is one of the most impressive women I've known.

One of my most treasured possessions is a red book titled "GiDeThloAhEe of The Blue People Clan." This book is about my family history and me. It also goes into detail about her many travels. She wrote this book for me as a Christmas Present in 1974. She passed away the following month on January 26, 1975, at 6:35 am C.S.T. There are only ten copies of this publication. One belongs to me; two are registered at the copyright office National Archives in Washington DC, and one at the Oklahoma Historical Society. One to the Cherokee Nation tribal attorney Earl Boyd Pierce, two at the Library of Congress, one to Steve Ralston, one to the Keetoowah band, and one to Mack and Fayeola Vann.

My aunt, a pillar of strength and resilience, had a contagious laughter filled with intense love. Many of you may wonder how I am so proud of her; I adore her with unwavering respect. I love her from the depth of my soul because I know she loved me more than she loved herself. You might be wondering how I came to this conclusion; well, I don't even know where to begin; I remember when my mom passed away, and I was in music class. The music class teacher wanted me to lead the song "Green Sleeves," for those who know the song, it is about a woman who passed away, and I just wasn't ready for that. The teacher decided to send me to the principal's office to be reprimanded, and back then, that meant a paddling, thankfully the principal knew my aunt, and he called her; she paid $5 to get to the school because we did not have a car so she had to pay for a ride so that she could talk with my teacher. I still remember her telling my teacher that I could kick her ass out of this state and back, but that's because she is my girl. If you lay a hand on her, if she gets a split end in your care, I'll cut your ears off if anything happens to her. Looking back on it, it's funny, but I'm pretty sure she meant it. She was always very protective, even in Church. There was a boy that lived in the house across the street from the Church, and we had a crush on each other, but I wasn't allowed to talk to boys; she grabbed him up by the ear, walked him over to his porch and told his grandmother you keep your boy on your side of the street and I'll keep my girl on my side of the street. If your boy comes to my side of the road, I'll give him an ass whoopin' he won't soon forget, and neither will you.

Sometimes it's not what you see, it's what you don't see, and it's not what is said; instead, it is the unspoken actions. There are moments in life when you must reflect within yourself deep within your soul and say to yourself; I can't hear your words because your actions are speaking so loudly. Her actions of love screamed passionately from the highest mountain in every expression of love she displayed for me. If there is one thing that you will take away from reading about my early years, I pray you will recognize your past does not define you. In life, you have a choice, either a victim or the victor; it is easy to become the victim and more challenging to overcome life's circumstances, but then again, I've always liked a good challenge.

I am very grateful for all these life circumstances because of these occurrences. I have a solid foundation of who I am, I am stronger because of these events, I have a solid emotional constitution, I have situational awareness that surpasses expected behavior, I have skill sets that no amount of money can buy, and no source of higher education can teach.

One thing that I did not mention at the beginning of this story of my early years is how my daddy did not speak, read, or write English. He could only say, read, and write in Cherokee, which means I am fluent and bilingual in both Cherokee and English. There were many times that because of this, what my daddy hunted was what we called dinner, and it was so much better than anything store-bought and, I'm pretty sure, so much healthier. My aunt could speak enough English to get by and often made a little money by babysitting. I'm proud of my daddy and aunt because they are the very definition of survivors.

I am very proud of the fact that I was born into the Keetoowah Nighthawk Society, I am from the blue people clan, and something just a little bit rare - I am accepted as part of the 49 rolls in the united Keetoowah band of Cherokee Indians. It is a birthright few people have today.

Time to Grieve

I am a blessed person, a child of God, just a little girl from Tahlequah. I hope that you will feel the pride that I continue to live in my Cherokee heritage as a Keetoowah Citizen; one thing you may not know about me is that I am the fifth-generation great-granddaughter of Sequoyah, also known as George "Gist" Guess, the creator of the Cherokee alphabet. I have a unique lineage that I would love to share with you another time because I believe this is an excellent place to start to share with you my journey to the White House. It all starts here, so I'd like to introduce myself properly, my name is Lisa, and it's nice to meet you.

I look forward to sharing my story with you, and I look forward to meeting every one of you so that you may share your story with me because a life worth living is a life worth writing about. Ironically, my journey didn't begin until my mother passed; they always say there is always a rebirth after a passing. My daddy used to say as much as I am his reason for being a better man, I am also my momma's phoenix rising from the ashes, breaking the silence, and building the foundation of a brand-new legacy washing away all the old.

I never really knew what he meant by that until other family members started sharing more and more with me about family secrets. My grandmother admitted on her deathbed that she killed a sibling of hers as well as one of her children, my aunt had also killed one of her children, a sibling, and then she had no other desire for more than her humble life, my mother used to wear a necklace that I never understood that had a date on it and on the front that read "a date to remember" and I later discovered that she had not only killed siblings as a child she had also done the same as an adult of two children, she was arrested for kidnapping, and that's just the tip of the iceberg. I think that's about all the secrets I want to share because I believe healing begins with forgiveness, gratitude, and the ability to put the past to rest.

In the Book of Life, God says that when you ask forgiveness, he casts your sins as far to the East as from the West. All sins are washed away, and the only thing left is the innocence that we were born with. In the Book of Life, the only story is forgiveness because he has washed away everything and made everything new. In my heart, I know they have all made peace because they all admitted to their wrongdoings on their deathbed, asking forgiveness, asking God's forgiveness, making peace with Christ so that they may rest in the glory of the Kingdom of God and how they must be celebrating.

I believe the day that my mother passed away was a new beginning; it was the day my journey began without me ever having any knowledge of the future and all the blessings that were yet to come, all of the treasures laid before my feet, all of the successes that I could never have comprehended. I always say if somebody ever told me this when I was ten years old or even eight years old, there is no way I would ever believe that it would be true; even if somebody told me this when I was 20, I would have never thought it because, after all, I am just a little girl from Tahlequah.

It was Friday, January 24, 1975, in the early morning hours. I was late for school. I had a few brief moments of a conversation with my mother. Never would I have realized this was the last day I would hear my mother's voice (I was eight years old, and she was 28 years old); only two days before she passed away to be with our Lord and Savior, I was waiting on the school bus wearing my favorite dress for school pictures, my mother called from Elko, Nevada after hitchhiking from Oklahoma to

Boston then onto Elko, Nevada and everyplace in-between; this was her second time to hitchhike across the united states. The first question she asked me was, "What are you wearing to school today?" I told her, "Your favorite dress, the one with the cherries. It's picture day, and I am wearing my tiara" We talked about school, she told me that no matter how different my aunt was, to have patience and behave for her; she told me she loved me in every way you could imagine and went on to say to me that no matter what else I remember the most important is to remember that God did not give us the ability to desire without giving us everything skills to achieve it and that Isaiah 55:11 is one of the most important verses to remember. My mother always said to be careful what you ask for because while you may not realize it, God is always listening, watching, and answering.

It's funny how you don't know any different when you don't know any different; whatever your reality is, you believe it is normal because you don't know any different. At that time, I thought we all lived in the same life circumstances with the same blessings and challenges without prejudice.

I never really understood why my mom needed to be constantly moving, always going, always doing anything other than being with family. At the same time, I always looked forward to hearing about her travels through conversations that I would listen to my aunt discussing with church members because everyone was always so curious about where she was and what she was up to.

As for me, at eight years old, I was still learning to be fluent in English because Cherokee was my first language. As I was learning to speak English in Briggs school, it felt like such a foreign language to me because the primary language in our home was Cherokee. It always has been and will continue to be because I am committed to keeping our language alive.

One thing that stands out in my mind about when my mother passed away was the conversations of people debating whether or not I should be allowed to see her at the Funeral Home. My daddy was the one who made the decision that I needed to be able to see her to have peace and closure; as hard as that was for me at the moment, I am very grateful for it today because it taught me the permanency of death and the celebration of life.

It taught me to be grateful for every moment that you are still breathing and every morning your eyes awaken; no matter what is happening around you, it's a fantastic, outstanding day. I may not always like what's going on in the moment, but when it's all said and done, I know that everything happens for a reason, and every sense is a design created by God for his greater purpose. We all make life decisions, and my daddy's decision to allow me to see my mom was the best, although painful as it was at the moment.

I still remember looking at her in the casket, believing that she was only sleeping, not liking the game she was playing because we used to play this game where she would keep her eyes closed and pretend to be asleep, and I would pull her eyelids open. I went to drop out of Daddy's arms to pull her eyelids open and tell her, "I don't like this game anymore. Please open your eyes, please," and Daddy pulled me back. Thank God he did because Lord only knows how many ways traumatic that could have been. You see, the thing is, the day that she passed away, nobody told me she passed away on that previous Sunday, January 26, 1975, and I didn't find out until Monday, the 27th, after school as the school bus was pulling down the road. My drop-off was about 1/4 mile from my house, and you could see cars lined up to the road, all quarter of a mile away, taking up both sides of the drive and the yard. There were so many cars you couldn't count them.

Coming from the culture and tradition I came from, that could only mean two things, either it was somebody's birthday or somebody had passed away, and I was banking on somebody's birthday; as I was getting off the school bus, I remember saying looks like a birthday is in full swing with anticipatory excitement of what was yet to come. When I got off the school bus, my daddy was waiting at the end of the road with my cat, Dan, and he picked me up. He put me on his shoulders, and he was carrying me through the cornfield just outside the watermelon patch; then I could smell the sweet, mouthwatering fragrance of the corn as Daddy told me, Baby, we need to talk, followed by Mom's not coming home. I promptly responded yes, she is, of course, she is; why would you say she promised and never breaks a promise? I was constantly defending my mom, maybe because I thought if I did it enough times, she would see how much I loved her and stay just once. Perhaps she would survive. Daddy said no, not this time. She's not coming home. She went to talk with Jesus. I responded, very matter-of-fact, that's okay. She'll be home as soon as she's finished talking with Jesus, not fully realizing what he told me. As it started to sink in, I remember going through many emotions, wondering why she would lie to me and asking Daddy why she lied to me; she told me she would never die. She told me she would always blow with the wind. Daddy responded profoundly: "Oh baby, don't you know she blows with the wind whenever you speak her name? She is blowing with the wind so sweet, sweet child of mine. She did not lie."

I greatly respect my daddy because he went above and beyond to protect me from pain and preserve my mother's memory. He always had a picture of my mother sitting out somewhere in the home throughout the years until the day he passed. That picture, that exact very same picture, is still the picture sitting out on my mantle because it meant so much to him. It means everything to me too.

The Reed & Culver funeral home flew my mother home to Tahlequah, Indian Country, Oklahoma, because my family had no means to bring her home.

Her Obituary read in the Tahlequah read,

"Mary Ann Eslinger was born "Sosti" Groundhog on Wednesday, October 23, 1946, to George Washington Groundhog and Sallie Ann (Dick) Groundhog of Tahlequah, Indian Territory U.S.A. She passed on Sunday, January 26, 1975, and was laid to rest on Thursday, January 30, 1975, at Cedar Tree Baptist Church.

Mary authored two books GI-Dee-Thlo-Ah-Ee of The Blue People Clan, for her daughter's 1974 Christmas present; Mary also wrote Cherokee People exposing the U.S. Government for their illicit exploitation and human trafficking of Native American girls.

Mary Ann Eslinger is survived by her daughter GI-Dee-Thlo-Ah-Ee Groundhog, Lisa Christine Christiansen.

Note: Recorded in "Our People and Where They Rest" Vol 10

Time To Grow

The year is now 1976, and my daddy married my aunt; Kenneth Littledave was the minister who officiated the wedding in our home, and he was also our pastor at Cedar Tree Baptist Church. At ten years old, it seems like I had already experienced more of life's celebrations and tragedies than most people will experience in their entire lifetime; I think the most important thing that happened during this year was the awareness that there are different socioeconomic levels of and how they affect families and their perceptions. It was the first year that I became aware that I was a Johnson O'Malley kid, I was also a C.C.F. child, which stands for Christian Children's Fund, and I think it was when I became fully aware of how hard my daddy worked to make sure that he provided for us through hunting because during these years much of what he hunted we called dinner.

Occasionally, we could go to the welling store, bringing me to my next growing experience. This event played a large part in building the foundation of my morals, values, and beliefs regarding giving to others and its impact on us.

My daddy used to make the absolute best butter and Jelly sandwich; yes, you heard that right, not a peanut butter and jelly sandwich, a butter and jelly sandwich, and it was always best served on store-bought bread for some reason in my crazy logic. There was a particular day that I walked to the old Welling Store to buy bread for my butter and jelly sandwiches (not peanut butter, butter.

my daddy made the best sandwiches); I still reflect on the day that changed my outlook on life as it happened in front of the welling store where my daddy loved to take me. How did this impact my outlook on life? You might be wondering, there was a woman with a child in front of the store needing just a little bit more money to have enough money for food, and how my daddy asked me to ask what she needed, remember we had only enough money for my bread. My daddy said you could buy your bread or give it to her. It's your money you decide. I really wanted my bread, but I always wanted my daddy to be proud of me; he said God always provides and rewards 10-fold, so because I wanted to make daddy proud, I gave her the money (all less than a dollar). Two weeks or so later, a man showed up at our house looking for a handyman (Dr. Bowman), and he brought with him more groceries than I had ever seen with more types of bread than I knew existed!!!...

That day changed how I thought about everything because at that moment, when I was a small child standing outside of the store with my daddy, God showed up, so I still give beyond my means, and God still blesses me beyond my needs.

My daddy taught me the power of a reality check. Take a self-inventory; how many boast about your Christianity because you sit in Church? The Church does not equal righteousness because authentic Christianity is only a relationship with God. How many of you plot revenge or even judge others because they sin differently than you? How many boast about forgiveness while complaining about things others pray for? How many of you say gratitude for your blessings as you miss out on opportunities to serve others? How many of you hold onto your last dollar rather than giving it to one in need because you can't afford to give? Guess what? You can't afford not to! How many of you look at a homeless beggar not seeing the person inside as you assume they must be an addict? It is not your job to judge; that's God's job. It is the foundational lesson I learned on that fine day at the welling store.

The old Welling store was a pivotal moment that shaped me into who I am today. This beautiful treasure off the beaten path in the middle of some-somewhere on the way to everywhere is a testament to how God puts you where you are intended to be in everything.

I say that because most people look at it as being in the middle of nowhere on the way to somewhere until you discover that this was your intended destination to receive God's gift that changes lives for the better through God's incredible grace.

Sadly, this beautiful little treasure closed 12 years ago, about the time I had been there last with my daddy, and gratefully, I have been abundantly blessed by this moment in time forever.

Sometimes I drive by this store and stop by and visit even though it's closed because it still holds many beautiful memories. Every time I visit, I feel the warmth and love of times long gone because it always reminds me to give beyond my means. After all, I know that God will always provide beyond my needs.

This store existed well into adulthood; I still remember my first car. I would visit the welling store to fill up with gas in my pink Corvette and buy some snacks, and many times Daddy and I would go back-road driving, and we would pick up sandwich meat, bread, and cheese. Not the fake stuff either, the real stuff, and there was nothing quite like a James Gaylor sandwich. He knew how to make a sandwich because it was always more meat than you would ever expect, and you could never finish the sandwich. They don't make them like that anymore.

These were the days when credit was your word, where you had a ticket, paid it on payday, and had no credit check. You would walk in, and they would write your access up; they don't have stores like that anymore; my daddy used to love going in there and charging for his ticket because it gave him a reason to go in and pay it, which meant he liked to socialize and then go on a back-road driving, I miss those back-road drives with my daddy on 100 highway.

When I was 13 years old, I saw a movie called Corvette Summer; it was a rerun, but it was such a great movie; I couldn't tell you what it was about. The only thing that I could say to you was when I saw that, I just knew that someday I was going to have a Corvette; I still remember telling my cousin that I was watching the movie that I was going to get a Corvette if it was the last thing I did and she looked at me like I had just grown a third head and said with what money, look around, we're never going to have anything like that. If we're lucky, we're going to have about nine kids and notice the order that I say this is because this is the order she said in.

She said we'd have about nine kids, we might get married eight or nine times, and hopefully, we won't get beat every day whether we need it or not. It could be more like once a week; look around. Who do you think you're fooling? Do you think you're better than us?

At that moment, as I was, I was sitting on the floor watching the movie "Corvette Summer," I thought to myself, I may not know what my life is, but "this is not my life"!!!... I wanted more, I wanted to be happy, and at that moment, a shift happened in my thought process because, at that moment, I knew that somehow, someday, that would not be my future.

I never wanted to be a nurse; I always wanted to be a doctor; I never wanted to be a paralegal; I wanted to be a lawyer with my law firm; I never wanted to be the secretary; I wanted to own the business; I made a decision that day that I would never work for anyone. I decided that day that I would own my own business, that I would own my product, that I would defy the odds, step up, set a new standard, and at that moment, I decided I would create an extraordinary life. I can honestly say with full transparency that everything I have most passionately and fervently wanted, God has given to me.

Be careful what you ask for because you will get it, and always remember to be mindful of your decisions because they will bear the fruit of your future and remember that to decide is to cut off, sever, and leave no other option or alternative.

Just remember the story of Troy because in the story of Troy, they built the Trojan horse from their ships, and with what was left, they burned their boats; they did this because they decided that they were fully committed to, and that is the best example of making a decision. If you're not fully committed to a decision, it's just an idea, and everything gets accomplished once it is made. Every decision and every action results in an outcome. It may be one you want, so choose wisely. I don't know how I knew this at ten, but I did because I grew up on dirt floors from birth through my early years. We finally had a house with wood floors.

I recall the home that was new to us because it was an upgrade, no more dirt floors and wood slats that are a child's dream because the aging, expansion, and contraction created foundations that you could see through. I recall how she would lay on the floor and watch the chickens run under the house as the cat would chase them. It was a simple pleasure that every child loved.

This home did not have plumbing or facilities. There was a pump well, a wood-burning stove for heat, and a wood-burning cook stove. An outhouse out back made for a luxurious life from previous experiences.

It was a two-room house overflowing with love, and somehow not enough for Mary Ann Groundhog Eslinger; she had bigger dreams with an appetite for success that matched only her ability to achieve her every desire and her unmatched determination to be in control.

We then upgraded to a different house, and when I was 16 years old, David, a gentleman who dated my mother, cosigned for my first vehicle only after telling me that he was giving me the gift of responsibility for my birthday.

David said he would cosign for any vehicle I wanted, the catch was I had to pay for it, and by this time, I was contracted with Ackerman McQueen out of Oklahoma City and partnered with Wilhelmina models; I didn't have constant work, but I did have consistent work, and I did get that Corvette for my 16th birthday it was my first vehicle. Right about now, as I sit here writing this, people go their whole lives to accomplish some of the things I completed just as a teenager, and we're just starting.

I think one advantage that I have isn't what people would assume; a lot of people believe that I started with money, and as you can see by my lineage and my history, I started with less than 0 financially, but at the same time where my advantage came from, I believe, is in the fact that in my personal opinion, I was already far more wealthy than anyone will ever be because I had someone believe in me, my daddy always believed in me when I told my daddy that I was going to get a corvette my daddy said: "oh that's great where's our first road trip?" He never had a single doubt that I would accomplish that, and you could even add David to that list of people that believed in me because he didn't have to cosign for that vehicle; he could have looked at me like any average teenager and thought that I would not have paid for it, but he believed in me and gave me a chance. I paid that car off and had that vehicle until I was 29 years old.

That's not the only time that David believed in me, he's one of maybe three people that didn't think I was crazy when I was invited to have lunch with Donald Trump on

April 15, 2010, and of course, I accepted the invitation, but we haven't gotten that far in the story yet.

You know, it's kind of crazy I never really did have any motivation or aspiration to be a model; I call it a God thing because of how it happened. Most people would call it an accident, but there is no such thing as an accident because everything is God's design. The photographer that took school photos had a stand-in photographer, and it just so happened that the photographer was a contributing photographer for Vogue magazine and Cosmopolitan.

He called my daddy and aunt for permission to do my headshots and contacted me with Ackerman McQueen and Wilhelmina. I started with local shoots like Dillard's and Montgomery Wards things like that, before ending up on the cover of Cosmopolitan and being highlighted inside of both Vogue and Cosmopolitan before I was even 17 years old, which a lot of young girls aspire to, for me this was just a part of the journey to get to where I wanted to be. It was just a means to an end because while I did enjoy modeling, I wanted so much more. I wanted to do something meaningful and impactful that would leave a legacy for generations to come, and this was simply a vehicle to get me there.

I'm abundantly grateful to God; I give all glory to God for providing me with every stepping stone that has gotten me to where I am today. One thing that I must say is that I indeed would have never believed that I would become an executive advisor in the Trump administration, I would have never thought that I would be a speaker of the White House, I would not have believed that I would be a part of such a historic campaign. That's also another story for another chapter.

You see, there's a reason that I knew I wanted something more that would leave a legacy for generations to come; it is because I have a lot to live up to and big shoes to fill. After all, if you go back in history, Sequoyah is my great-grandfather from 5 generations ago, and he created the Cherokee syllabary; in other words, he's why we have a system to communicate. A gentleman by the name of H. A. Scomp, A member of Emory College faculty, declared that "perhaps the most remarkable man who has ever lived on Georgia soil was neither a politician, nor a soldier, nor an ecclesiastic nor a scholar, but merely a Cherokee Indian of mixed blood. And strange to say, this

Indian acquired permanent fame, neither expecting nor seeking it".

You see, Sequoyah was the son of a Virginia fur trader. He was born in Tennessee; what makes this important to me is my daddy would hunt and sell the hides at the sale barn on Saturdays, which is the same thing as being a fur trader, at least to me. Sequoyah left as a youth and removed to Georgia. There he worked as a silversmith; Sequoyah did not sign his works since he did not know how to write. He began to study how to spell his name, and in 1809 he began working on a Cherokee writing system.

He was just a man with a dream and the determination to bring this dream to fruition because, at Wilson, Alabama, he enlisted in the Cherokee regiment fighting in the battle of horseshoe bend, effectively ending the war against the Creek Red Sticks.

During the war, he became convinced of the necessity of literacy for his people, our people. He and other Cherokee could not write letters home, read military orders, or record events as they occurred. I can appreciate why he felt it was necessary to have our system of literacy because, without that ability, we were at a disadvantage in many ways; we were at a disadvantage because there was no way to record history as it was happening, we cannot communicate with family members, a simple luxury really and at the same time an absolute necessity as proven by history itself. I can only imagine how this idea was born and the myriad of emotions that flooded his soul to bring forth the vision and strength to bring this to reality, especially with everybody fighting against him, telling him that it was a ridiculous idea, which they did, some even called it witchcraft.

After the war, he developed a phonetic system where each sound made in speech was represented by a symbol. He created "The Talking Leaves," 86 letters that comprised the Cherokee syllabary. Later, a publication began on the first Native American newspaper, the Cherokee Phoenix.

Today his syllabary is still being used and is an essential part of our language preservation to the point that we have immersion schools to keep our native culture, tradition, and, most important, our native tongue alive.

If you think about it, Sequoyah did something quite extraordinary, the written form of the Cherokee language introduced by Sequoyah happened in 1921, and it offered its people a bridge between prehistory and modernity.

Sequoyah also left us treasures beyond measure through his originally allotted land throughout Oklahoma and on my mother's side of the family, which is how I relate to Sequoyah. We still hold sacred, and I still reside with humble gratitude on the part of the original allotment of Sequoyah's land.

I still reside in the house that I grew up in even though it has been moved several times and rebuilt at least twice; I say that because this house is actually not the same because it started with dirt floors, and we even had an outhouse before we got an upgrade to the place that I was telling you about with the wood floors that had the slats in it where you could feed the chickens under the house through the bottom, I can't tell you how exciting that always was, I love chickens.

Because of a fire, the house was restored in the 1970s, and I recently did my restorations of this beautiful sacred two-room home that I love with all my heart.

When I say I have big shoes to fill, it doesn't end with Sequoyah. My grandfather on my mother's side was a pretty amazing person, too; as I sit here, about to share an article written recently about my grandpa.

I am somewhat speechless because I am humbled in ways that I've never experienced, grateful to levels that escape words; I find myself searching for ways to impress upon you just how unique each of you is and how easy it is to take for granted our family history.

Sometimes my life is just like everyone else's, pretty standard and average, even until that moment of curiosity brought on by a series of unexpected events. I received a phone call from a very impressive journalist, asking how much I remembered about my grandfather, my mother's father. There isn't much that I don't know because we were so very close and as close as we are because I was so young. I don't think I fully grasped just how much of an impact my grandfather made and continues to make today in our tribe, traditions, culture, and lives.

I want to thank this impressive journalist R. E. "Eddie Glenn," the Tahlequah Daily Press, and their magazine, the Tahlequah Grapevine, for this outstanding, extraordinary article on my grandfather and the opportunity to share memories with our great tribal nations and the world at large through this book.

Some people may not even know what a code talker is, but my grandfather was one of the last surviving code talkers. In the military, they enlisted Native Americans of many different tribal nations to create a way to communicate without the enemy being able to decipher the message because during World War II, sending and receiving codes without the risk of the enemy decoding the transmission required hours of encrypting and decrypting the code.

The U.S. marine corps enlisted Navajos as the first code talkers, with other tribes being brought in succession. My grandfather's name is George Washington Groundhog, one of the most extraordinary men I know; I am proud that he is my grandfather.

He was an army veteran of World War II and served in Rhineland alongside General George S. Patton. That's impressive. I'm not the only one who thinks that my grandfather was so amazing; the army did too because he was decorated with three bronze star medals, a "V" device that distinguishes heroism or valor in combat, a World War II victory medal, a combat infantryman badge first award, an honorable service lapel button WWII, and two purple hearts.

I mentioned these things first, but this is nowhere near the most impressive thing he's ever done; he has many tools in his belt of accomplishments.

It is no wonder that my mother was such a fighter for the rights of others because after he finished fighting World War II, he came back to Oklahoma and is very well known to this day as the leader of "The Fight That Influenced Five Nations" my grandfather came back and founded the OCCO and just in case you do not know what the OCCO is this is the acronym for the original Cherokee community organization.

You see, in the summer of 1969, W.W. Keeler was facing one of the biggest challenges of his then 20-year stint as principal chief of the Cherokee Nation. A group called the original Cherokee community organization had filed a lawsuit in federal court, calling for the removal of Keeler as chief and the election of tribal leaders by Cherokees themselves rather than being appointed.

The tribe had not held elections since the Curtis Act of 1898, and a subsequent series of similar federal laws had ended Cherokee governance.

That same series of laws had implemented the Dawes rolls census of tribal members in the land allotment system. Thus, Cherokees and members of the other Five Civilized Tribes - the Muscogee (Creek), the Choctaw, the Chickasaw, and the Seminole- became land-owning citizens of the United States and the state of Oklahoma.

With the beginning of statehood in 1907, chiefs of the Five Civilized Tribes were appointed by the U.S. president. This chief-naming responsibility the federal government reserved for its executive branch was facilitated by transferring any tribal lands that had been overlooked during the land allotment process.

Keeler had distinguished himself at Phillips Petroleum during World War II by overseeing the construction of a refinery in Mexico that helped Allied forces keep their planes, tanks, trucks, and other military vehicles fueled by moving forward against the Italian, German, and Japanese troops. He developed relationships with government officials during that time, and in 1949 was named by President Harry Truman as principal chief of the Cherokee Nation.

That sort of federal involvement in tribal affairs, however, did not sit well with George Washington

Groundhog, founder of the OCCO. Like Keeler, Groundhog played a critical role in the success of Allied troops in World War II.

He had served in the United States Army as a code talker, using his native Cherokee language to befuddle any German troops who might be listening to American radio transmissions. Many Germans could translate English, but finding a German soldier who could understand Cherokee or any of the other native languages used by code talkers, was virtually impossible.

In the decades following the war, the Cherokee language and traditions remained vital to Groundhog's identity. By the late 1960s, he had become frustrated with the Keeler's lead collection of businesses identifying as "Cherokee."

Using some of the $14.7 million he had helped acquire in a lawsuit against the federal government for lands wrongfully opened to white settlement in 1893, Keeler set up several Cherokee businesses, including the Cherokee Cultural Center and a tribal newspaper, Cherokee Nation News. To Keeler, those businesses facilitated Cherokee's participation in the larger American economy. Groundhog saw them as an extension of the federal government and Euro-American values, Cherokee in name only. In this article written by Eddie Glenn, during the interview with me, I told him I have vivid memories of my grandfather's views on the importance of the Cherokee language and culture.

He believed there was a defining line between the Indian and white worlds. When I was a little girl, he would take me fishing. We might not catch anything, but we would talk in Cherokee while we fished, and if I asked him a question in English, he would answer when I asked him in Cherokee.

Many Tahlequah residents will know the oft-heard Cherokee greeting, "Osiyo." They may recognize the initials of the original Cherokee community organization, OCCO, when babbled, as very nearly as an interlinguistic pun on that greeting. Intended as an acronym or not, the initialism OCCO does represent everything Groundhog saw in the anthesis to the Cherokee identity espoused by Keeler, whose concept of Cherokee identity was corporate-based and future-oriented.

In a speech in October 1969 to the Texas manufacturers association, Keeler described Cherokees as "building a new and vigorous nation with the goals of bringing the economic benefits of modern America to our people."

On the other hand, my grandfather George Washington Groundhog saw Cherokee identity as community-based espousing traditional tribal values and, most importantly, the Cherokee language. Quoted in the August 19, 1969, edition of the Cherokee Nation news, Groundhog said, "Keeler was unqualified to lead the Cherokee people because he doesn't speak Cherokee." The paper- which, keep in mind, was founded by Keeler- proceeded to suggest Groundhog and the OCCO held anti-American views.

"Some mixed-bloods and newspapers in northeastern Oklahoma have hinted that the OCCO has held secret meetings resembling communist cell meetings of the 1930s," the author of the story about the OCCO's lawsuit wrote. "One government official, who asked to remain unidentified, termed the OCCO movement "part of a big plan on a multi-front level attempting to take over the Negros, Cherokees and Indians and peoples to gain control of the governing powers of the United States."

Those were some serious allegations to make against my grandfather George Washington Groundhog because he was a decorated soldier injured in combat, a fighter, a force for good. However, such insinuations indicate the acidic nature of the Groundhog/Keeler dispute. On October 21, 1969, edition of the Cherokee Nation news, Keeler said, "I've been trying to get an election of the chief since 1954. But the act of Congress ties us into the other four tribes. Some of the tribes want an election; others don't. So, you have a prolonged procedure to convince Congress that elections would benefit the Cherokees."

Keeler may have been advocating for tribal elections for years, but Congress didn't even consider a bill allowing such polls until after the OCCO's lawsuit was filed. Introduced by Oklahoma congressman Ed Edmondson on November 5, 1969, H.R. 14676, also known as the Principal Chiefs Act, called for a change in federal policy to allow members of all Five Civilized Tribes to choose their leadership.

Archived correspondence of both Edmundson and Keeler indicate the two were close friends and that Keeler contributed significantly to the wording of the bill. For example, Keeler proposed that the legislation be worded to allow the five civilized tribes to "select" rather than "elect" their leadership because he claimed, "some of the tribal groups said they did not want to hold elections as they could be costly and could dissipate tribal funds at the expense of important programs."

Edmundson corresponded with OCCO members about the bill, writing to OCCO secretary Luella Pritchett in December 1969 about the progression of the bill through Congress: "I am enclosing a copy of my account on this subject, H.R. 14676, in hopes that it will be of interest to you.

The house interior committee will be able to begin hearings on the bill as soon as possible. If there is anything else that I can do to be of service, please don't hesitate to let me know."

Congress passed it in 1970 and signed it into law by President Richard Nixon. The principal chiefs act ultimately brought about modern democratic Cherokee governance. Despite his lack of popularity with some more traditional Cherokees like Groundhog, Keeler was elected as the tribe's first popularly chosen leader since 1903. Under his leadership and that of his successor Ross Swimmer, a tribal constitution was ratified by Cherokee voters in 1976.

The OCCO's lawsuit against Keeler was eventually dismissed, but to say Keeler won and Groundhog lost would be ignoring what appears to have been a crucial impetus for congressional consideration of the Principal Chiefs Act - the public dissent exhibited by the OCCO. If there's a lesson to be learned from the OCCO, sometimes being a thorn in the side of authority might yield remarkable results.

One thing that must be said about my grandfather, George Washington Groundhog, is that he was very committed, and if he was fighting you, he was going to fight you to the bitter end; when he believed in something, he was with it all the way.

My grandfather passed away on February 18, 1979, and Keeler eight years later.

Though the legal, cultural, and linguistic disputes between the two may be relegated to the rarely revisited recesses of history, they likely significantly impacted the life of every native tribal member in eastern Oklahoma. Talk about some big shoes to fill, and now we're just getting started.

I know you might be wondering just how this has anything to do with my journey to the White House; well,

I want to impress upon you that I am just a little girl from Tahlequah. a simple girl from a family with humble means and the tenacity to fight for what they believe in.

As Daddy says, "You don't have to stand tall, but you do have to stand up, don't ever start the fight, but you better damn well finish it."

I am just an ordinary girl, a little girl who once upon a time couldn't see past the dirt floors of Cherokee County, never expecting that my life would find its way from the tiny little two-room house without running water and an outhouse to the White House.

My story inspires you to reach for your dreams, dream so big that it scares you, and hold on to that dream.

Do you want to know how to become a champion? It's easy. Turn your dream into your goal. Plant it deep in your heart, then eat, sleep, breathe, laugh, and cry without ever taking your eye off your plan, not even for a second, because an obstacle is what you see when you take your look off your goal. Focus with laser-like precision, and your brain will become a servo mechanism to achieve your outcome.

Remember that your resolution to succeed is more important than any other. Remember, if you do not prioritize yourself, how can anyone else? When you've thought about everything and that good idea shows up, write it down and run with it. Take up one picture. Make that one idea your life, think of it, dream of it, work for it, and live on it.

Let the brain, muscles, nerves, and every part of your body, be full of that idea, and leave every other picture alone. It is the way to success.

Vision comes in many shapes and many forms; there is the kind our vision our eyes afford us, there's the kind of vision our wisdom gives us, and there's the kind of vision that comes from things sensed, things dreamt, and then there is the kind of vision that comes from patience and persistence. Vision is a gift of God's knowledge placed deep in our hearts, planted to be nurtured until it bears fruit for harvest to become the bounty of our labors. For this reason, you must create your vision to act upon because your wave of action, however insignificant you may see, becomes an unstoppable force. Make sure it is the outcome you desire.

With all the chaos and uncertainty we face in our lives and this world, have you taken your self-inventory today? I surrender no power to be held over me other than giving to God, which is all of me and what he has in his plans. I am sure only that it is for the greater good of all. My uncertainties do not rule me, nor do I allow them to control me. I live well and plan as best as possible; I do not dwell on uncertainties.

As you come to know me better, I hope that you will feel the pride that I have lived and continue to live within my Cherokee heritage. I stand for what I believe in even if it means I stand alone because if it's worth considering, it's worth fighting for, and who I am is a child of God first.

People get so caught up in what race they claim when the most critical D.N.A. you should be concerned about is whether or not you are a child of God.

My specialty is not as a teacher but as a follower because I would instead follow the example of Christ rather than lead by ignorance.

Today life is excellent as this morning I woke up and accepted my blessing from God to have this day.

I choose to share it in his name with all this world and his children. I am excited about my life, my career, my success, my strength, my energy, and my optimism. I am proud of myself and my influence to help others achieve their outcome and own their future. I am excited to enrich the lives of others. I believe everything happens for a reason.

Everyone is good at the core level, and I trust more often than not. I know that everything works itself out. I live in gratitude and forgiveness, my gifts are faith and contribution, and I believe love will always find a way. I always have.

I have found in my life through my experiences that the only thing that separates us from animals is our ability to have emotions, none of which that I have experienced would I classify as typical.

You must always make your decisions with the end in mind and know you are guaranteed an outcome. Be wise in your choices, for they will be your fruits.

Of all the roads traveled, there is no right or wrong path to cut, as they all lead you to where you are meant to be. I have traveled many roads and cut many courses—some unorthodox and most conventional. I will not try to fit in when I know in my heart God has meant for me to stand out! I am enough for God, and that is enough for me.

I will not apologize for my decisions or the events in my life, as they have made me a woman of integrity with the gift to accept others for who they are now and love them without prejudice.

Will you choose to follow the road of others, or will you cut your path? Will you allow your past circumstances to hold you back from your deserved love, wealth, and success? Choose and be happy!

I do believe that God places us where he needs us for his more excellent design because, through all of these life events that I have shared with you, one thing that holds is I wouldn't change anything if God stood before me and said, "I will allow you to change anything in your past, and it shall be done" I wouldn't because I do believe that everything that happens brings us to where we are in this moment, I think that every decision we make builds the foundation of our character, creates the integrity of our morals, values, and beliefs, it shapes us into who we are and into who we are yet to become, and because I am so abundantly grateful for my life I wouldn't change a thing.

I have two beautiful daughters that are self-sufficient, self-sustaining, productive members of society, and that's more than most people can say. My eldest daughter went to College at the University of Arizona and then continued to get her doctorate in Native American Art history at the University of Illinois. My youngest daughter owns two businesses: tailor-made tattoos and a dog training service. Both of my girls are very successful; I couldn't be prouder.

That's not to say that they didn't have their ups and downs in their teenage years, as most do; I'm reasonably sure that all teenagers go through a stage of self-discovery, and in those moments, they can be a challenge. I think of these times as God preparing us for the day; they are ready to move out and become the best version of themselves.

I say this because I have experienced many facets of life, placing me on the Mary Kay path. I know what you're thinking; Mary Kay is just a multi-level marketing company that you can only make money doing consistently. Well, that's just not true.

When you are placed in a position to do Mary Kay, which is your only income, it becomes sink or swim, do or die;

it is your livelihood; I promise you he will find a way or make way for it to succeed.

I was invited to a Mary Kay party like most people are. As I was sitting there, I wasn't focused on the skincare class as much as I was focused on how a 5-year-old with good directions could do this job, and with that, I decided I didn't have anything to lose because, at that point in my life, I had just come out of a divorce. I did not have any other source of income so for me. It was a good idea; I would be okay with being out of the $107 it took to start the business. I still remember having to borrow that $107.00 from David because, as I said, I had just come out of a divorce, so I didn't have any money; I was starting from scratch again.

Around that time, I was making starting over a hobby, not purposefully. I was determined to make this work, and make this work I did. I came into the company of Mary Kay somewhere within the last two weeks of March 2004. Within my first month, I had made over $32,000 collectively; in June, just the month of June, I made $22,342. Yes, you read that correctly. That earned me the title of head of state and the highest income earner in the entire nation for June and July.

I stayed with Mary Kay for five years, and I loved it; I loved the friends I made, I loved the product, and I loved almost everything about it; about the only thing that I didn't love was the jealousy that I believe was happening from my upline because somehow everything that I did upset their apple cart.

I still remember the day that I got a call from my immediate upline who told me that it was company policy not to promote above your upline, funny thing about that is when you go to a meeting, they say, "We encourage you to surpass us, because the more you make, the more, we make" I guess I took that literal. They said that Mary Kay was about enriching the lives of others in my upline. They meant that they believed in improving the lives of their selected few because I received a letter from corporate that insisted no, demanding that I slow down my sails or resign my consultantship.

I'll never forget the day I received that letter because I called David, he didn't live very far away, maybe 3 miles, and I had been crying so much that all I could muster up to say was, please come over. When he arrived, the first thing out of his mouth was what happened because he knew it was obvious. My whole body was shaking; I had been crying myself into exhaustion because, for five years, I had become a success story of Mary Kay. I couldn't understand why they wouldn't want to utilize one of their best assets, one of their highest income earners. I couldn't decide what to do; I had won many awards and bonuses and perfected my "I story " and" why story. Mary Kay teaches you to stand in front of a crowd and speak to the fruition of your ultimate vision. Now I bet you're wondering why I'm telling you this story about Mary Kay and my vision statement; it has everything to do with my journey to the White House.

My vision statement is headlined in the journal that Mary Kay gives you, and the heading of it starts with "my biggest career vision as I now see it." There's a space, a page for you to write your vision statement, and this was mine: I am a multi-million-dollar national sales director with $1,000,000 directors in my national area.

I am known for having a dream that reality has continued to exceed every day. I bring the vision to fruition to all those with integrity and motivation. I say yes to my goals when everyone else says no.

I invest in others and their dreams; I build people and teach them to do the same. I own investment properties and rentals throughout the country, including Hawaii, where I also own a winter home. I am the new Mary Kay! I am so excited and so grateful because, within five years, I will meet and take a picture with Donald Trump; I will get an autograph and a testimonial because I am a child of God.

Keep in mind that the vision statement was written in 2006; in 2010, I received an e-mail from Melissa Lopez, and because that e-mail was sent on April 1, 2010, I thought it was an April fool's joke because the subject line read "Would you be available to have lunch with Donald Trump on April 15", that's tax day, now you can see why I thought it was a joke.

I thought that was the best April Fool joke anybody has ever pulled. Then I read the e-mail, she had two phone numbers attached to that e-mail along with great detail, and I figured I had nothing to lose and everything to gain because if it wasn't true, I already thought it was a joke. If it was true, I couldn't even imagine the possibilities of how that opportunity would shift my life in directions that I could have never seen coming, not even with my vivid imagination.

I called Melissa Lopez, and we had a lovely conversation; she told me that she would e-mail me the questionnaire that I would have to write an essay, a 500-word essay because Donald Trump was choosing 15 people from across the United States to meet with in New York City and from those 15 people only a few would be selected. I was so nervous; I told her I was a speaker, not a writer, and she encouraged me to complete the questions and do my best. We were on a time crunch because I had seen that e-mail on the 10th which left little time.

On the 12th, I was on my bicycle in the refuge when Melissa called me. My hands trembled as I saw the phone call coming in, and somehow, I didn't think I was chosen. She asked, "Are you sitting down? It sounds like you're riding your bicycle," I said, "I am riding my bicycle, so technically, I'm sitting down. Don't worry about rejection, we're on a first-name basis. We are real good friends."

She responded with, "I think you need to sit down and at least unclip," for those of you that don't know what unclip means if you are a cyclist, you do know if you are not a cyclist, unclip means when you're in clipless paddles, you're locked in, and if the bike goes down you're going down.

I unclipped. I stood on the side by the country corner where I had good reception, and she said Lisa, you're going to New York City. You were chosen. I don't know how many ways to describe how excited I was at that moment, how grateful I was, and how grateful I still am. The worst thing that could happen is I wouldn't get chosen, but I went with three outcomes in mind I wanted to get a photograph, an autograph, and a testimonial for my website.

So, you can imagine my excitement knowing that I was about to fly to New York City to meet Donald Trump, who I consider the most intelligent businessman ever; I was so excited I couldn't believe it. I had to call everybody that I knew to tell them.

How did that work out for me? Nobody believed it was real; everybody told me it was a scam, I would be kidnapped, and there was no way I had anything to say that he would need to hear. It would help if you were more intelligent to work with or for him. Honey, I heard it all.

Only two people believed in me; they were the only two who thought it was a good idea for me to go to New York City. Chris Silva was skeptical; he said so you're flying to New York because you talked to a woman that claims to work for him, and you're just going to trust that she's telling you the truth because, of course, you know her after all, you met her on Facebook.

In Chris's defense, I know he was looking out for me, and he was concerned, so he did his homework, and after much deliberation, he decided that it might not be my worst idea. Still, it wasn't my best idea; I just needed to be careful.

I appreciate that because I know I tend to be very optimistic, and he tends to be incredibly pessimistic, so it was a good balance. On the other hand, David was excited for me; he told me I hope you can get everything you are determined to return with. I hope you take a photo with him and get a testimonial, and I hope he takes the time to answer your question. So, I can say that David just went on absolute blind faith to the point that he even gave me the money for my luggage to get on the plane; he even drove from Oklahoma City to Lawton, OK, to go me to Oklahoma City to the airport so that I could fly out on time I was so nervous, scared, I had so many emotions floating around, and there was a small part of me that was genuinely praying that this was real, that this was happening to me because, after all, I'm just a little girl from Tahlequah things like this don't happen to ordinary everyday people.

On April 14, 2010, I flew to New York and stayed at the Trump Soho, which no longer exists. The experience cannot be put into words after the meeting at trump towers on the lower level right under the escalator, where he announced his candidacy for President.

I walked up to him and tapped him on the shoulder so nervous because I had no idea how this was going to go, but I figured the worst that could happen was he could say no, and I just thought, well, that's not so bad because once again rejection and we're on a first name basis.

Nothing could have prepared me for what was about to take place next. He turned with kind eyes, and I asked, "I have three requests. Would you consider taking a photograph with me, answer one quality question, and possibly get a testimonial because I have tremendous respect for you" This was in the day of the BlackBerry, and that's all I had with me, so I didn't expect to get outstanding photos, I would have been thrilled if I would have just had photos that you could tell who he was, and so I handed my BlackBerry to a nearby person. I asked, "Please just take as many photos as you can. All you have to do is point and click. Just take as many photos as you can please."

He was so kind and so generous with his time, he said sure what's the question, and I responded, "Well, I do public speaking, sometimes I have a crowd of 2000 people, and sometimes I have a group of 10,000 people and my quality question I would like to ask is how do I reach the maximum amount of people in the shortest amount of time so that they hear the message in a way they need to listen to it because I feel like some people are not focusing on the news.

I feel like some of the women would place more value on hearing the information from a man, while I feel like some of the men can't get past the fact that I'm a woman, so I'm not feeling they are listening to the message as much as they are focused on the package."

He jokingly said, "That sounds like three questions; you are a brilliant woman, so stop focusing on the ones who do not believe what you have to say; some will, some won't, so what.

Some will leave, and they will make room for the ones who genuinely need your help and authentically want to learn and grow their business, relationships, and life. Stop focusing on trying to hold on to the ones who don't want to be there. Focus on the ones showing up for themselves, and success will follow." I also got a testimonial for my website, which was priceless because you can't pay for that advertising. I wasn't prepared for Denise Winters of Denise Winters Photography to be there and capture this art in motion as Donald Trump, and I were conversing; she captured this candid shot.

It isn't where my interaction ended, and I only want to share this because many people have a distorted opinion because they don't know him. They haven't seen him personally, so I have a little patience in withholding my defense mechanism because Donald Trump is truly a man who is family oriented. He is a man who wants to leave a legacy of kindness. He wants to leave this world a better place than when he came into it. He wants to provide for his family. Hence, they never have to struggle or worry.

Many of you think that is a given because of who he is and what he has, but the man I met wants to leave a legacy much bigger than the almighty dollar.

He is a man that impressed me in ways that reminded me very much of the way my daddy lived his life because I saw him with my own two eyes give money to someone struggling outside of trump towers, and he didn't just give him pocket change, he gave him a couple of $100 at least. Another thing that truly impressed me was how there were construction workers near the area that had nothing to do with Trump Towers. They were not working on anything that belonged to him, and he went out and introduced himself; that in and of itself is impressive; the other thing that impressed me is he remembered each of their names.

He took them coffee and was very prompt to let them know that he had made arrangements for them to be able to have lunch in Trump Towers.

He did not know anybody saw this, so I feel privileged to have witnessed such kindness that exceeds expected behavior. It is a side of Donald Trump that people don't see; they automatically assume he's the character on television with the "you're fired" attitude. Here's what gets me about picking your favorite movie when you watch a movie. Do you seriously think the person playing a particular character behaves like that character?

I wish everybody could see the kind, gentle man I saw on April 15, 2010, because that is a man with integrity that exceeds anyone's expectations. This is a man with unparalleled character because I was always taught that character is defined by how you treat somebody who can do nothing for you; your character shows up when you have extraordinary acts of kindness when no one else is watching. He is the Donald Trump I met on April 15, 2010.

The date is now June 16, 2015, only five short years after my first meeting with Donald Trump, he announced his candidacy for the presidency of the United States of America.

I did not know this; David leaned over the railing of my then-home and said, "Your boy is running for President," Now this could mean a lot of things because Lance Armstrong is someone that I look up to in cycling and consider both Lance and George Hincapie mentors. I also admire and appreciate Chris Carmichael, as I look up to him as a mentor.

In my opinion Donald Trump is the best businessman ever and one of my "why" statements it actually reads "I am the Donald Trump of women in business" so that kind of says it all.

My immediate response to learning of Donald Trump's announcement to run for President Of The United States of America was a very selfish one because I had never paid attention to politics.

I don't know that I ever thought that my vote even counted.

Something shifted that day when David said, "Donald Trump is running for president" the first thought that went through my head was "Do you have any idea what this means to me, that testimonial that I have instead of it being a testimonial from the greatest businessman of all time it will actually be a testimonial from the president of the United States of America that is definitely advertising that you cannot pay for." After listening to his policies, I decided to pay closer attention because everything he spoke about, I was completely in alignment with, and he may very well be the best president of all time ride alongside Ronald Reagan.

I can say with full transparency I have never stayed up all night long to watch the polls to see who the next president of the United States of America would be but this time I did, and the excitement was overwhelming because I had never been so invested in an election.

At this point I was truly invested in the election for unselfish reasons because I really did believe that he could make a difference, he could make a change, I knew that he was the best person for the job because while everyone was telling me that he was a businessman and had no business being president of the United States of America my response was "he's exactly the man for the job because of the fact that he's a businessman because after all the United States of America is nothing more than a big corporation and who better to run it than a businessman, and certainly in my opinion the best business man of all time."

I respected his Christian values which mean so much more to me than what anybody could ever realize, I respect his family values, and I respect the fact that what you see is what you get. I heard so many people criticize him for being too blunt, to Kurt, some people said that he had no tact. In my opinion that's what made him a great president and that's what makes him a great man because I would rather hear the cold hard truth than the sweetest sugarcoated lie and with Donald Trump, he's not afraid to say what he means and he means what he says, that's something to be respected in a time where people lack respect.

This attitude earned me a position on the campaign trail, never in my life would I have ever believed if somebody would have told me that I would be involved in the political arena in any capacity so you can imagine my surprise and excitement when I was called upon to work the campaign.

I consider it one of my greatest accomplishments, I am truly honored and humbled that anyone would even think of me for such a position to be a small part of something so monumental, I was invited to the inauguration and the inaugural ball as a VIP guest, David leaned over the banister when he heard me get that phone call and he with great surprise said only you, this could only happen to you.

I was excited and crying at the same time as I told David I can't believe this, I really just can't believe this because I'm just a little girl from Tahlequah if anybody would have ever told me that this would be my life when I was 10 years old never in a million years would I have ever believed this, and David responded I know, you're just a little girl from Tahlequah as he jokingly teased me and told me I'm proud of you.

I can't tell you how much this affected both my daddy and me because so many people were against the fact that we were supporting Donald Trump, there was even an article written that was titled "Last Monolingual Cherokee and Daughter Are Under Fire for Supporting President Donald J Trump".

When my dad heard about this he said "baby don't back down, stand up even if it means you stand alone. You don't have to stand tall, but you do have to stand up.

I'm standing right beside you" I did go to the inauguration and the inaugural ball.

I invited a young man by the name of Shane Bouvet because he reminded me of myself, I know that I would not be where I am had others not taken me under their wing and brought me along and lifted me up.

I felt it was my responsibility to do the same for Shane, I am so proud of Shane because he is such a good, good man. When we were in Washington DC Donald Trump gave him a $10,000 check the day before the inauguration and he gave every bit of that check to his dad fighting cancer. Shane Bouvet is wise beyond his years; he has integrity and character beyond his years because most people of his age more than likely would have spent that money selfishly, but he gave every bit of that money to his daddy.

He worked so hard on the campaign, he spent his own money to purchase Flyers, stickers, political collateral to hand out using funds from his own pocket while raising his son.

He is an outstanding human being, a great father, and a good son. I chose wisely and we are still very good friends and I'm guessing we are both working on the campaign for the next election. After the election we continued to work, I spoke at the white house twice, I spoke during the March for trump events, I had the honor and the pleasure of attending numerous events as one of the few Presidential Advisory Board members. Not too bad for just a little girl from Tahlequah.

I am looking forward to a future of success supporting the Trump family.

Living a life living in the gratitude of wealth on so many levels, living a life that I once believed to be a dream".

On a personal and spiritual level I would like to remind you of a few simple yet easily forgotten truths to which I say, God, thank you for making me see so clearly.

When I was a little girl I had dreams so much bigger than I could ever be, dreams of leaving Tahlequah and traveling the world, dreams of success and things, lots of things, and somehow I just knew I was going to make everything happen.

My daddy (<u>Mack Vann</u>) always told me that the greatest riches were sitting right here in front of me, I never really did understand that remark.

My daddy was always proud of me and I'm pretty sure I could do no wrong in his eyes, I was always the apple of his eye, daddy's little girl, daddy's little princess. I still remember when a lady at church called me spoiled and my daddy never did get over that, ever.

I still remember the day she passed away and he refused to go to her funeral as I sat dressed up waiting to go and attend and pay my respects reflecting on how he told her that's not called spoiled that's called loved.

As I sit here today with my cup of ginger tea sitting in my tiny little two room home which I guard with all my heart, as I have a cup of tea sitting in front of me, I reflect back on those words so long ago that my daddy said how the riches were right in front of me.

Guess what, he was right, as I look around and realize that of all the roads traveled and all the paths I've cut, of all the countries I've visited, and from East Coast to West Coast and everywhere in between the greatest riches really are right here right in front of me as the birds sing in the trees and the memories of everything daddy and me did here in this tiny little two room house.

Everything from fixing water lines, laying the gas pipes, chopping wood, and building memories, these are the foundation of life.

No greater riches are there then those found in the memories with my dad.

When you're out there building your success take a moment to reflect, make certain to remember so many people get caught up in the everyday hustle and bustle, they spend their whole life building a business, don't get so busy making a living that you forget to make a life.

Interview with Shane Bouvet: A Guiding Light in the Shadows

In the midst of the intricate narrative woven throughout the story, one individual's influence stands out as a guiding light amidst the shadows. I had the privilege of sitting down with Shane Bouvet, a man with an unwavering spirit and steadfast integrity, who emerged  from the pages of the campaign trail to leave an indelible mark on my journey. In this exclusive interview, Shane shares his perspective on his unexpected role in shaping the path of justice.

Q: Shane, your journey from small-town blue-collar life to becoming a volunteer coordinator for a presidential campaign is both inspiring and unique. Could you tell us about your experience and what motivated you to get involved?

A: Absolutely. You know, I was just a regular guy living paycheck to paycheck, trying to make ends meet for my son and myself. The prospects of life outside seemed distant until I found myself delivering signs for Donald Trump's campaign. There was something about the promise of change that resonates with me, and I knew I wanted to be part of it. Little did I know that this decision would lead me to become a volunteer coordinator and propel me onto a journey that touched lives in ways I could have never imagined.

Q: Your involvement in the campaign took an unexpected turn when you became the volunteer social media coordinator. How did that happen?

A: It's quite a story. My dedication to this campaign didn't go unnoticed, and soon enough, I found myself coordinating social media efforts in Illinois. It was a leap of faith, but I believe in the cause and wanted to be a voice for those who often went unheard. I realized that social media was a powerful tool to reach out, connect, and mobilize people who share our vision.

Q: Your character's dedication and integrity shine through, much like my journey in the novel. How do you see your journeys intersecting with the themes explored in the narrative?

A: It's humbling to think that my journey resonates with the themes of justice, integrity, and dedication that run through the novel. Just like your relentless pursuit of truth, I was driven by a desire to bring positive change to corners of the country that had been forgotten. My involvement wasn't just about the campaign—it was about believing in the potential for renewal and healing in places like my hometown. It's about standing up for what's right and lending a voice to those who may not have the chance to be heard otherwise.

Q: The story captures the essence of the human spirit and the impact of personal connections. Could you share a moment from your journey that reflects the power of these connections?

A: One moment that stands out is when I met Donald Trump during the campaign. He signed a campaign sign for me and acknowledged the effort I had put in. It was a brief encounter, but it left a profound impact on me. It made me feel like I was part of something bigger—a movement that aimed to make America great again. This connection gives me the motivation to keep pushing forward, no matter the challenges.

Q: As the story concludes with renewed determination, where do you see your journey leading next?

A: My journey has instilled in me a deep sense of responsibility to continue advocating for change and justice. I want to be a catalyst for positive transformation, just as your character is in the novel. My work doesn't end with the campaign; it's a continuous journey of making a difference wherever I can. I'll keep using my voice, standing up for those who need it, and seeking justice in my way.

Shane Bouvet's story mirrors the themes and values that define the novel—a journey of seeking justice, embracing transformation, and standing up for what's right. As his voice intertwined with the narrative's essence, his character serves as a reminder that even in the shadows, there are those who illuminate the path of justice and integrity.